TEACHING
ENGLISH

TO

SPEAKERS
OF ENGLISH

TEACHING ENGLISH TO SPEAKERS OF ENGLISH

BRADFORD ARTHUR

University of California, Los Angeles

HARCOURT BRACE JOVANOVICH, INC.

New York   Chicago   San Francisco   Atlanta

Cover: Portions of compositions written by students in elementary schools in Los Angeles, California, and the Bronx, New York.

ISBN: 0-15-588211-2

Library of Congress Catalog Card Number: 73-1795

Printed in the United States of America

for Kathy and Jeff

PREFACE

For the past eight years I have taught a basic English linguistics course that is generally required of students training to become public school teachers. At first I followed a conventional syllabus: one unit on phonology, another on syntax, a third on language history, and some concluding remarks on the role of linguistics in the schools. Occasionally, when I was in the midst of explaining distinctive phonological features, or the passive transformation, or Grimm's law, some impertinent student would interrupt to say in effect, "That's all very interesting, but what good is it for an English teacher?" I found such questions somewhat annoying, probably because I was never satisfied with my own answers.

Belatedly, I began to take this type of question seriously and, as a result, soon started a search for better answers. As I learned more, my replies became more elaborate, and the syllabus of my course focused increasingly on subjects central to the concerns of teachers rather than on those primarily of interest to linguists: for example, the nature of language attitudes and prejudices and their effect on education, the linguistics of reading and writing, the teaching problems created by the diversity among English dialects, and the evaluation of proficiency in language skills. Ultimately, my thoughts on these and similar subjects became both the core of my syllabus and the foundation of this book.

I wish to acknowledge my debt: to hundreds of my students whose needs encouraged me and whose questions and insights guided me; to the UCLA TESL faculty, who taught me respect for applied linguistics, and especially to Riley Smith, Evelyn Hatch, and Sandra Garcia for conversations that gave shape to many of the ideas in this book; to Jean Wilkinson for careful and sensitive reading of an early draft and for good advice unselfishly and tactfully offered; to Carolyn Johnson, who edited the manuscript with skill and care that taught an English teacher humility; to Marika for years of patience, prodding, and proofreading; and finally, to my children, Kathy and Jeff, whose language learning experiences I have exploited ruthlessly. They gave me the joy of hearing language grow.

BRADFORD ARTHUR

CONTENTS

6 EFFECTS OF DIALECT DIFFERENCE IN READING AND WRITING 99

7 RECOGNIZING AND CONTROLLING SENTENCE DIFFICULTY 119

8 TEACHING ABOUT LANGUAGE 141

TEACHING
ENGLISH

TO

SPEAKERS
OF ENGLISH

INTRODUCTION

Educational planners responsible for the training of elementary-school, secondary-school, and junior-college English teachers have come to recognize a need for more extensive teacher training in the area of English linguistics. One of the most authoritative statements of this need is in the report of a study sponsored by the National Association of State Directors of Teacher Education and Certification, the National Council of Teachers of English, and the Modern Language Association of America and published in 1967 under the title "English Teacher Preparation Study: Guidelines for the Preparation of Teachers of English."[1] Three of the six guidelines presented in this report specify the primary-school or secondary-school English teacher's need for training in linguistics. Guideline II states: "The program in English . . . should provide a balanced study of language, literature, and composition above the level of freshman English." Guideline IV states in part that "the teacher of English at any level should have . . . an understanding of the nature of language and of rhetoric." Such

---

[1] "English Teacher Preparation Study: Guidelines for the Preparation of Teachers of English, 1967," *PMLA* 82, no. 4 (Sept. 1967). Quotations below are from pp. 22–25.

"understanding of the nature of language" is then analyzed in greater detail:

> He [the teacher of English] should have a well-balanced descriptive and historical knowledge of the English language.
> 1. He should have some understanding of phonology, morphology, and syntax; the sources and development of the English vocabulary; semantics; and social, regional, and functional varieties of English usage.
> 2. He should be acquainted with methods of preparation and uses of dictionaries and grammars.
> 3. He should be well-grounded in one grammatical system and have a working acquaintance with at least one other system.
> 4. He should have studied basic principles of language learning in order to apply his knowledge at various grade levels to the problems of those learning to speak, listen, read, and write to a variety of audiences.
> 5. He should have an understanding of the respective domains of linguistics and rhetoric, and of the range of choice available within the structure of the language.

Guideline V, which describes the need to provide English teachers with an understanding of "the relationship of child and adolescent development to the teaching of English," indicates that one area of child development important for the English teacher is language development:

> He should have studied the language development of children and adolescents: their interest in language, their growth in using vocabulary and syntax, in understanding and using figurative speech, as well as their growth in the ability to distinguish among several varieties of usage.

These guidelines, if followed, would change drastically the distribution of courses taken by most English-teachers-in-training. At present, however, rather than undertake the balanced study of language, literature, and composition specified in Guideline II, the prospective teacher of English is likely to enroll in a large number of upper-division courses in English and American literature and few, if any, upper-division courses dealing specifically with English linguistics. This lack of balance may be attributed in part to a scarcity of available instructors for English language courses, but also, perhaps primarily, to the attitude of prospective English teachers toward linguistics courses. Students preparing to become teachers of English may be motivated by a desire to serve society, a love of children, an interest in literature or creative writing; but rarely does anyone preparing to teach elementary-school or secondary-school English begin with a serious interest in language study. Far more typically, teacher trainees know little and care less about English linguistics. Many never did study grammar (since in many high schools only those students with special "writing problems" have to study grammar). Many prospective teachers whose interest in English reflects a humanistic rather than a scientific bent are distressed by the increasingly mathematical and "scientific" aura that surrounds linguistics. Consequently, teachers tend to view the one required English linguistics course with a mixture of dread and resignation.

The study of grammar holds a hallowed spot in the school curriculum as traditionally conceived: teachers expect to teach it and students expect to study it. Too seldom do teachers or students ask *why* it should be taught. When they do ask, they are generally told that students must know grammar if they are to speak and write English properly. This statement is often followed by a series of examples illustrating the deplorable state of English composition nowadays. Incomplete sentences and run-on sentences abound; modifiers are often misplaced or left dangling; and sentence structure frequently becomes so garbled that ideas are obscured rather than expressed. Such problems need curing, and most teachers have always prescribed a good dose of English grammar.

Teachers who accept this application of English grammar in English classes are distressed by the seemingly perverse way in which linguists keep changing the rules of grammar. Just as teachers recently adjusted to the "new math," so periodically must they adjust to a "new English." The changes are so rapid that a teacher may find that the grammar he is teaching his seventh-graders is different from the one they learned in the sixth grade.[2] Such teachers come to view linguists as separated into particular camps, each pitted against the other for the minds of American youth. Thus it is now fashionable to ask: Which grammar—traditional, structural, or transformational—should be taught in the schools?

[2] For the past several years the texts adopted by the state of California to teach English grammar at the upper elementary level have differed in terminology and to some extent in underlying grammatical theory from the state-adopted grammar texts for junior high schools.

This question is a product of two sorts of misunderstanding that exist between educators and linguists. First, many of the educators who have asked it have not been aware of the range and nature of the actual differences and similarities among linguistic theories. As a consequence, minor differences have been exaggerated and important ones ignored. Educators often contrast methods of diagramming or labeling parts of sentences without mentioning or even understanding the more fundamental differences in purpose and approach that caused linguists to invent new terms or to re-define existing terms. Moreover, underlying the debate among educators over approaches to grammatical description is an assumption as to why linguistics is important for education: linguistics is supposed to provide a set of grammatical rules which, when taught to students, will improve those students' language skills. But linguists do not write grammatical rules with this end in mind, and most linguists find this use of grammatical rules questionable.

If formal instruction in grammar is not an efficient or appropriate cure for bad writers, then why should English teachers teach it, and still more fundamentally, why should they have to learn it themselves? The guidelines quoted at the beginning of this chapter suggest something of an answer. They imply that teachers who understand the early language development of children will better understand their students' ability to learn language-related skills in school. English linguistics is important in school *not* because it can be taught to third-graders but because it offers teachers a clearer understanding of how a third-grade student uses language and how this use of language affects his ability to read, to write, to understand what is being said, and to say things clearly to a variety of audiences. Teachers with a new understanding of language-related learning skills are better equipped to develop new teaching techniques or new diagnostic procedures; they can offer new hope to those "problem students" whose language differences would otherwise cause them to be shuttled through the public schools without really learning how to read or write. A teacher may or may not decide to explain to his class the relationship between language-related subjects and the structure of language, but he should certainly understand that relationship himself.

Obviously, the more teachers know about the English language and English linguistics, the greater will be their potential for applying linguistic concepts in teaching language-related skills. But a knowledge of linguistics is only of value to teachers who also understand the nature and limitations of its application in their field. Introductory and advanced textbooks in linguistics abound, many written specifically for teachers; but teachers need and cannot find a theory suggesting how current linguistic conceptualizations of English and of language in general can be applied to classroom activities—like teaching students to read and write better.

Such a theory of applied linguistics must not be based on a utopian view of teacher training in linguistics. Most teachers are and must continue to be trained as generalists rather than as professional linguists.[3] Linguistics is only one of the disciplines contributing to their competence, and not the most important one at that. (If it comes to a choice, let teachers gain a coherent philosophy of learning and a psychology of motivation and skip the linguistics.) A practical theory of applied linguistics for English classes must be able to guide even those teachers who are, from a linguist's point of view, grossly undertrained—teachers who have had that one required English linguistics course or less.

This book is one linguist's effort to provide such a theory. It is not on the one hand an introduction to linguistics nor on the other a guide to classroom procedures and techniques. Rather, attempting to fill the gap between the purely theoretical and the purely practical, it provides the classroom teacher with a set of principles for using linguistics in devising and evaluating teaching techniques. The book is thus meant to be within the understanding of linguistic beginners; and linguistically sophisticated readers are asked to be tolerant of whatever oversimplifications occur in the text in the attempt to incorporate basic information about language and linguistics.

A brief summary of the topics covered in subsequent chapters will suggest the range of applications linguistics can have for English teachers. Chapter 2, "Natural Language Learning," presents some special learning principles that distinguish language learning from other types of learning. This chapter also suggests how these principles can lead to more effective teaching techniques for such

---

[3] The ideal training program for English teachers mentioned at the beginning of this chapter would include no more than four or five English linguistics courses: one or two courses treating the structure of English sounds, words, and sentences; a course in social and regional dialects of American English; an introduction to theories of language learning and language development; and a history of the English language.

areas of language learning as the development of vocabulary. Chapter 3, "The Linguistics of Reading," suggests some ways in which teachers can use a knowledge of linguistics to teach reading strategies and evaluate the extent to which students are able to employ such strategies. Chapter 4, "The Linguistics of Writing," offers linguistic explanations and remedies for many of the difficulties that students typically have in mastering composition skills such as spelling and punctuation. Chapter 5, "Language Attitudes, Language Variation, and Standard English," presents a linguist's view of style and dialect difference. This chapter also suggests some ways in which teachers can lead their students to a mature knowledge of formal, standard English and to mature attitudes toward style and dialect variation. Chapter 6, "Effects of Dialect Difference in Reading and Writing," suggests teaching responses to the special set of learning problems that confront students whose dialect is considered "nonstandard" and inappropriate for use in the classroom. Chapter 7, "Recognizing and Controlling Language Difficulty," offers teachers some techniques for evaluating the difficulty of English sentences and for simplifying the English language in response to the needs of students who are not yet fully in control of it. Finally, Chapter 8, "Teaching About Language," describes some of the reasons why a teacher might want to teach students about their language and how teachers can go about presenting the English language as subject matter. The remaining sections of this first chapter outline certain principles of language learning which are fundamental to the discussion in the chapters that follow.

Active and Passive Language Skills

Anyone who knows English is both a sender and a receiver of that language. He knows a system of associations between ideas, thoughts, feelings, desires, concepts—the whole range of phenomena we call meaning—and the complex arrangements of vocal sounds we call English speech. In addition, the speaker of English knows how to use these associations to convert meaning into vocal sounds, and, conversely, to convert vocal sounds into meaning.

The following diagram represents this two-way association between meaning and sound:[4]

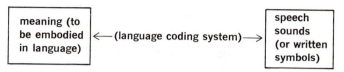

In their attempts to describe this coding system, linguists have noted a separation of the total system into three component systems. The first of these component systems contains rules governing the association of meaning and sound without representing the procedures whereby this association is used to express or understand meaning. This first component system has been called linguistic competence. Linguistic competence does not characterize

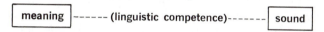

specific paths between meaning and sound but instead provides rules and information necessary for blazing or following such paths. It provides a basis for speaking and understanding language in much the same way that the rules of chess provide a basis for playing the game but do not themselves constitute or describe the innumerable games of chess that have been, will be, and can be played following those rules.

Chess games proceed in only one direction, from the initial positioning of the pieces on the board to the checkmate; language moves in two directions, however, from meaning to sound and from sound to meaning. Moreover, the procedures to be followed for moving in one direction are neither the same as nor simply the reverse of the procedures for moving in the opposite direction. Movement in each direction is governed by a separate component system of procedures or strategies.

[4] The box shown on the left-hand side of the diagram represents meaning apart from language. This convenient simplification of the meaning end of the language coding system begs a fundamental philosophical and linguistic question: Can meanings be formulated without some form of language? Can we ever completely disentangle our thoughts from some sort of linguistic embodiment? But if meaning is inseparable from language, how can a bilingual reexpress meaning from one language in another without abstracting such meaning from its embodiment in either language?

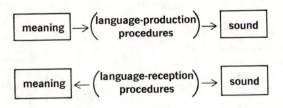

When a speaker wishes to express some idea, he must search for and piece together words and phrases that will constitute the verbal expression of his idea. He is, in a sense, trying to match a pre-existing idea with some sequence of words. A speaker of English wishing to talk about his occupation might select the word *engineer* as an element in his message. This process of word selection requires a knowledge of English (linguistic competence) that includes: the mental equivalent of an English dictionary; a system of semantic relationships possible between words; and a system of correspondence between semantic relationships and such overt grammatical markers as word order, intonation, and inflection.

The word *engineer*, together with the other words in the message, would be received by some other individual who would then face the different task of reconstructing the original meaning from its expression in the language code. The receiver would begin not with ideas but with words. His task would be to determine somehow which of the conceivable messages is embodied in the words. Receiving the word *engineer*, he would have to use his skill as a language receiver together with his linguistic competence to determine whether *engineer* referred to an action or to an individual; if an individual, whether it referred to a locomotive driver or a bridge designer; and whether that individual was the receiver or performer of some action expressed elsewhere in the message.

In this example, the process whereby the speaker selects the word *engineer* is different from the process whereby the receiver discovers its meaning. And neither of these two processes is the same as the knowledge of the language code (linguistic competence) existing in the minds of both the speaker and the hearer. What makes this whole language process wondrous, fascinating, and extremely puzzling is that neither the speaker nor the hearer is conscious of how he is going about the task of selecting and arranging words to convey meaning or of deciphering words as representing meaning. Both processes occur in an unconscious split second.

Based on this view of the language "process," it is natural to separate those language skills involving a movement from sound (or writing) to meaning from those skills employed in moving from meaning to a spoken (or written) representation of that meaning in English. Because speaking and writing involve some muscular activity as well as mental activity, they and comparable language skills are referred to in this text as *active*. Since hearing and reading are physically, although certainly not mentally, passive, they are referred to as *passive* language skills. These two labels identify two different, complex, largely unexplored sets of mental processes. Fortunately for teachers, the ability simply to distinguish these two sorts of language skills, even without a deep understanding of their nature, can provide important clues as to how school-age children learn language and why they learn it as they do. Such information can lead in turn to a more fruitful encouragement of this learning process.[5]

Learning How and Learning About

A teacher spends part of his time teaching students *how* to do things and part of his time teaching students *about* things. When teaching *how*, his objective is to provide students with the capacity for a new type of behavior, with the ability to perform or to act in a new way. When teaching *about*, his objective is to instill new knowledge, new understanding, or increased awareness.

The following statements describe acts of teaching *how*:

1. A child is taught how to ride a bicycle.
2. A dog is taught how to heel.
3. A student is taught how to look up words in a dictionary.
4. A trumpeter is taught how to triple-tongue.

[5] For a more elaborate discussion of the distinction between active and passive language and implications for second-dialect teaching, see Rudolph C. Troike's "Receptive Competence, Productive Competence, and Performance," in James E. Alatis, ed., *Monograph Series on Language and Linguistics*, no. 22: *Linguistics and the Teaching of Standard English to Speakers of Other Languages or Dialects* (Washington, D.C.: Georgetown University Press, 1970), pp. 63–69.

And these describe some instances of teaching *about:*

1. Civil War buffs are constantly looking for someone or some book to teach them more about the Civil War.
2. The popularity of fan magazines and gossip columns suggests that much of the public is anxious to learn more about the private lives of famous people.
3. Archaeologists study ancient ruins to learn more about former civilizations.
4. You are now being taught about the distinction between teaching how and teaching about.

The distinction between teaching *how* and teaching *about* applies as well to the teaching of the language arts. A child entering the school system must learn *how* to: read, spell, punctuate sentences, use different styles of English fluently and appropriately, write and speak clearly, coherently, and convincingly on a variety of topics; and must master many other language skills as well. If a student enters the school system without the ability to speak English or able to speak only a dialect of English unacceptable in the schools, he faces the task of learning *how* to speak a new language or dialect. Students are learning *about* language when they learn, for instance, that *curfew* originally meant "cover fire," that English is an Indo-European language, or that the interrogative pronoun *who* has an objective form *whom.*

The surest proof that someone knows *how* is to watch him perform; the surest proof that someone knows *about* is to listen to him explain. Indeed, the ability to explain what one knows is entailed in knowing about it. *Knowing about* something, as that term is used here, means possessing conscious knowledge which can be verbalized or in some way explained to others. Not all forms of knowledge can meet this criterion. We may know that we love or hate someone, but we may not be able to explain precisely what feelings lead us to this knowledge or what characteristics in the individual generate our feelings. Many religions also claim to be based on knowledge that cannot be expressed or explained, maintaining that the knowledge which comes through enlightenment cannot be conveyed through explanation but must be acquired instead through various forms of religious exercise, meditation, or prayer.

The line between knowledge held consciously and knowledge that cannot be raised to the level of conscious thought is often difficult to determine. A beginning musician just learning how to read music is generally conscious of how the pitch and duration of musical tones are represented by notes written on stafflines. But, when continued practice brings greater fluency and speed, such conscious awareness is superseded by unconscious habit: the eye sees the note on the page and almost simultaneously the finger moves to depress the appropriate key on the instrument. The advanced musician may concentrate on how to get the phrasing just right, but he certainly does not consciously think about which key to press.

Ordinarily an advanced musician's knowledge of the relationship between notes and keys is not conscious to the degree a beginner's is; this knowledge can, however, be recalled to consciousness. When asked, the skilled musician can still explain the system of musical notation although he no longer concentrates on it as he plays. Such *knowing about* musical notation must be considered "conscious" for two reasons: first, the principles of musical notation were originally learned consciously; and second, the musician whose knowledge of musical notation has reached the stage of automatic habit can still bring his knowledge back to consciousness and describe or discuss it if he wishes to do so.

Neither of these two criteria for conscious mastery is met by first-language learners. At no time during first (that is, native) language learning is the learner consciously aware of the rules he is following in speaking and understanding—although no linguist doubts that any language user's knowledge can be expressed, in part at least, as a set of grammatical rules. Neither the child at an early stage of language mastery nor the linguistically mature adult can raise the elaborate system of the grammatical rules he follows to the level of consciousness required for *talking about* (and therefore, in the sense defined above, for *knowing about*) these rules.

Most speakers of English can talk about individual sentences but not about the grammatical relationships and processes occurring in these sentences. They can explain, for example, what a sentence like *Dorothy found the Wizard of Oz* means and what most of the individual words within it mean (little words like *the* and *of* are usually the hardest to define), but unless some teacher has broken the news to them, they are not consciously aware that *Dorothy,*

Wizard, and *Oz* are members of the same class of words (noun) while *found* is a member of a different class (verb). In addition, they are not consciously aware that *Dorothy* and *Oz*, following a general rule for proper nouns, do not take the articles *a* and *the*. Everyone who speaks English, however, unconsciously classifies words in this way when producing and understanding sentences. That is one reason why *the found of Oz* and *Wizard of the Oz*, sound strange. But knowing that such sequences of words sound strange is not the same as being able to explain *why* they sound that way.

First-language learning may be unique among intellectually based learning in that the learner does not know and never did know *about* what he is doing. Unfortunately this special characteristic of language learning is generally ignored when language skills are taught formally in school. Students are taught a second language, or more formal styles of a language they already speak, in much the same way they are taught to read music: by first consciously learning *about* grammatical rules and practicing them, hopefully to the point where these rules become an unconscious part of a developing language system.

A language teacher is in a special position: the skill he teaches is one that students are capable of learning without his professional help. A non–English-speaking child approaching school age can learn English by spending six months in the midst of English-speakers; and he can learn it so well that his command of the language will be virtually indistinguishable from that of his exclusively English-speaking peers. Such second-language learning occurs whenever a child participates regularly, even for a few hours a day, in a community where a language other than his own is spoken: no formal instruction is required. Unless a language teacher is able to improve on a child's natural ability to learn language, formal instruction may hinder rather than aid the learning process. To state this notion in a slightly different way: a student can be learning language skills even when the teacher is failing to teach them.

Thus, the first-language or second-language teacher is accountable in a way that the social studies, math, or music teacher is not. He must gauge his success by determining not how much was learned in his class but how much *more* was learned there than could have been learned elsewhere—without formal interference in the learning process. One of the principal arguments advanced in this book is that English teachers improve the efficiency of their instruction when their teaching techniques build upon and act in harmony with, rather than hinder, the natural capacity human beings have for learning language.

Children, especially, are capable of mastering some language skills without first learning *about* the principles of language underlying those skills. In order to build upon this natural capacity to learn language, however, the teacher must know which of the language-related skills taught in school are controlled by natural language-learning ability and which are not. Moreover, the teacher interested in encouraging natural language learning within the "unnatural" confines of the classroom must understand some of the principles by which such learning operates and upon which new teaching techniques can be based. This book was written to introduce teachers to some of the basic principles of natural language learning and to suggest how such principles lead to new techniques for teaching English language skills.

NATURAL LANGUAGE LEARNING

A science teacher might want to teach his class *about* the process of digesting food, but no one would or could teach *how* to digest food. Digestion is an ability that people are born with, like blinking, sneezing, and crying. Many more activities are partly but not entirely governed by inborn talents. For example, the baseball coach may teach his players how to throw a baseball more accurately or more rapidly, but the ability to throw objects comes to them naturally as it does, in varying degrees, to all people. Even before a child is able to walk, he can pick up objects within reach and throw them out of reach. Indeed, as any mother who has spent hours picking up toys and putting them back into a crib can testify, babies have natural throwing arms. Natural body functions such as the digestion of food and psychomotor skills such as jumping, kicking, and throwing develop wholly or in part in response to innate predispositions.

In learning the more intellectual and conscious skills needed to function within his environment and culture, however, the human learner seems to be guided not by elaborate, inborn blueprints, but by a set of general learning procedures involving trial and error, reward, reinforcement, and generalization. Until recently, most linguists would have accepted these general learning procedures as adequate to account for language learning. Clearly, a language learner is responding to cultural and environmental stimuli: language learning requires a language to be learned, which implies the existence of a speech community. A child raised apart from human society and culture would learn to walk and kick and throw objects like other human beings, but he would not learn to speak a human language.

However, in spite of this obvious dependence of language learning on the learner's cultural and social environment, many psychologists and linguists have come to believe that special innate talents make a child's language learning different in kind from the learning involved in the rest of his acculturation and socialization. This new view of language learning as governed in part by special innate learning procedures or talents has far-reaching implications for the language arts teacher. Teaching methods that are appropriate for most other subject matters may not be appropriate for language-related skills. If language arts teachers are to develop different, more appropriate teaching methods, they must recognize and encourage their students' special natural talents for language learning.

At least three sorts of evidence suggest that every child brings into the language community a set of highly specialized talents for acquiring human language. First, there is the fact that success at language learning is virtually universal. All healthy children begin learning language during their first and second years of life regardless of whether parents encourage, ignore, or even discourage the learning process. And, on a larger scale, no culture in the world is without a language. The languages of so-called primitive cultures are structurally no less sophisticated than the languages of more technologically advanced cultures.

Second, language learning proceeds in a natural developmental sequence. Just as they acquire certain basic psychomotor skills at roughly the same ages and in the same sequence, children acquire different language skills in a predictable order and at a predictable age. The parallelism of these developmental sequences is illustrated in the following chart:

CORRELATION OF MOTOR AND LANGUAGE DEVELOPMENT

Age (years)	Motor milestones	Language milestones
0.5	Sits using hands for support; unilateral reaching	Cooing sounds change to babbling by introduction of consonantal sounds
1	Stands; walks when held by one hand	Syllabic reduplication; signs of understanding some words; applies some sounds regularly to signify persons or objects, that is, the first words
1.5	Prehension and release fully developed; gait propulsive; creeps downstairs backward	Repertoire of three to fifty words not joined in phrases; trains of sounds and intonation patterns resembling discourse; good progress in understanding
2	Runs (with falls); walks stairs with one foot forward only	More than fifty words; two-word phrases most common; more interest in verbal communication; no more babbling
2.5	Jumps with both feet; stands on one foot for one second; builds tower of six cubes	Every day new words; utterances of three and more words; seems to understand almost everything said to him; still many grammatical deviations
3	Tiptoes three yards (2.7 meters); walks stairs with alternating feet; jumps 0.9 meter	Vocabulary of some thousand words; about 80 percent intelligibility; grammar of utterances close approximation to colloquial adult; syntactic mistakes fewer in variety, systematic, predictable
4.5	Jumps over rope; hops on one foot; walks on line	Language well established; grammatical anomalies restricted either to unusual constructions or to the more literate aspects of discourse

Source: Eric H. Lenneberg, "On Explaining Language," *Science*, 164, no. 3880 (May 9, 1969), p. 636. Copyright 1969 by the American Association for the Advancement of Science. Reprinted by permission.

This type of regular developmental sequence correlated with age is characteristic of skills that develop in response to biologically controlled maturational timetables; but it is not characteristic of learning that is controlled primarily by external teaching and encouragement. The timing and sequencing of this second type of learning depend in part on the timing and sequencing of the external encouragement and instruction, and are therefore much more subject to variation. A child's notion of what is linguistically correct and appropriate seems to be determined as much by his own linguistic intuitions as it is by the linguistic data he receives from adults and older children. Consequently, in the face of adult interference, children are often vehement in their determination to follow their own speech norms. And some children have even been known to "correct" their parents' speech.

A third and final reason for considering language learning in part the product of an innate language-learning capacity shared by all human beings is the fact that all human languages, in spite of their obvious superficial differences, have a great deal in common. The type of abstract grammatical rules necessary to describe one language are identical with or very similar to the rules needed to describe any other naturally occurring human language. This fact has led some linguists to conclude that the rule system itself is in some sense innate and that different human languages merely represent different manifestations of this same underlying system.

Since language develops naturally and at a fairly consistent rate among preschool children, the elementary-school teacher can assume that his entering students have already attained a predictable level of language proficiency and that they will continue to increase this proficiency in predictable ways and at a predictable rate. If the teacher knows the extent and nature of the linguistic knowledge a child brings into class, he can more intelligently decide what language skills they should be taught as students. Teachers who are unaware of the developmental sequence in language learning may attempt to teach language skills that students have already acquired or are not yet prepared to acquire. It seems useful, therefore, to consider at this point some of the language skills that children possess by the time they are of school age.

In several important respects children have already learned their native language by the age of four or five years—that is, in most cases, before they begin to attend school. By this time they have trained themselves to distinguish whatever differences in speech sounds are used in their language to differentiate one message from another; moreover, they have also learned how to make all or nearly all of these contrasts in speech sounds. School-age children have active control over all of the major word or morpheme classes in their language.[1] They have mastered the inflectional system whereby English verbs are marked for tense and nouns are marked for plural number, and they can distinguish various parts of speech, not only the major classes, such as nouns and verbs, but also such subclasses as animate and inanimate nouns and transitive and intransitive verbs. Before they are enrolled in school, children have also mastered the system of rules governing the pronunciation of those morphemes and words they know. Only the unsystematic or "exceptional" words—such as the past tense forms of irregular verbs like *go* or *think,* or the irregular plural forms of nouns such as *man, person,* and *deer*—may still give them some difficulty. At school age, children are already able to recognize and produce grammatically correct sentences in their language. They can make statements and ask questions, use imperative sentences to command and negative sentences to deny. They have mastered the rules for using conjunction or one of the various forms of subordination to create a long sentence out of shorter ones. They know how to implement the rules for shortening a sentence by deleting redundant words and phrases. Finally, they are capable of using this complex linguistic system to communicate their ideas, feelings, and desires and to respond to the ideas, feelings, and desires of those around them.

However, in spite of his impressive language-learning achievements, the language skills of the preschool child do not meet the linguistic demands of adult society. As a child's range of experience

---

[1] The morphemes of a language are the smallest units of meaning recognized and used by speakers of that language. Morphemes cannot be considered the same as words since frequently words contain more than one morpheme. The word *rejoined,* for example, contains three morphemes, the first meaning "again," the second meaning "unite" or "attach," and the third meaning "past tense." Nor should the concept of a *morpheme* be confused with that of a *syllable* since some morphemes, like *elephant* and *English,* contain more than one syllable. Moreover, morphemes cannot always be associated with particular segments of the spoken or written words in which they occur. The word *went,* for example, contains two morphemes—one meaning "proceed" or "move," the other meaning "past tense." However, neither of these two meanings is confined to a specific set of sounds or letters within the word.

grows, so too does his need for words and sentence structures with which to describe that experience. To say that the preschooler already knows his language certainly does not mean that he commands a range of vocabularly and syntax adequate to adult needs. School systems have traditionally assumed the task of teaching children new words, but vocabulary development by itself will not prepare a child to assume adult language roles. He must also learn to control a wider range of language styles or registers. The auxiliary verb *got* as a marker of the passive voice (it *got* broken) must yield in more formal speech or writing to some form of the verb *to be* (it *was* broken). In the same way, *gonna* must, upon occasion, yield to *going to*, and *who*, under suitably pretentious circumstances, must yield to *whom*. Of course, no teacher should become so overzealous in his determination to teach formal, "correct" English that he ignores the student's need to understand and use a wide variety of different styles. Another aspect of language learning that can be encouraged and directed by teaching is the development of new linguistic strategies. Though they have never been adequately catalogued, there are definitely strategies for telling someone he is wrong without saying it in so many words, for complimenting or congratulating, for commanding, for consoling, for capturing sympathy, and for confusing. Children use the direct approach: "Give me the sugar," or "You're a liar." Adults have learned some more subtle, less antagonizing strategies for getting the same points across: "Can you reach the sugar?" or "Perhaps you are mistaken."

The speech of school-age children differs from adult speech for several reasons. First, the natural language-learning sequence described in this chapter is still in progress when a child becomes four or five years old, and additional language skills must await further maturation. Second, children entering the school system are still at an intermediate stage in their general intellectual development. The changes in a child's language during his years in elementary school reflect this continuing intellectual development. The average length and syntactic complexity of his sentences increase as a child moves through elementary school and then through secondary school. Certain grammatical constructions, such as the past perfect tense in English, are rare in the speech of elementary-school children. These constructions are difficult for the young student more because of the complexity of the concepts they involve than because of the complexity of the language necessary to express them. Third, a young child lacks the range of experience upon which an adult knowledge of language must be based. He has been exposed primarily to the casual or intimate language appropriate for conversations with parents and playmates. He does not control the more formal styles of English which are appropriate in the classroom and in written expression. Similarly, the limited size of the vocabulary a child acquires by school age reflects in part the limited range of his experience. Finally, the dialect that the child has mastered before entering school may be different from the dialect he will be expected to use in the classroom. This is obviously true of many minority-group children, but in less obvious ways and to a lesser degree it is true of all children. For example, when a young child uses the past tense form *brang* rather than *brought*, or *won* in sentences where an adult would expect *beat* ("I won Billy at checkers"), he may simply be following the speech norms of his peer group. His playmate Billy and other friends may use these same words, and the "correct" adult grammar may be considered incorrect within their group of friends.

In teaching vocabulary, formal style, or linguistic strategies, the teacher should realize that he is at most encouraging a natural learning process that would occur even without formal pedagogical assistance. He must face the possibility that by interfering with his students' acquisition of language-related skills he may be hindering rather than helping their language development. In evaluating his own teaching methods he must, therefore, ask not only whether these methods are better than other methods he might use, but whether they are better than simply leaving the language learner alone to acquire language skills without interference.

Thus far this chapter has presented reasons for considering language learning "natural" and for taking this naturalness into account in the design and evaluation of programs to teach language-related skills. Before continuing with this discussion, however, it is important to consider two major limitations that the enthusiastic teacher should keep in mind. Language-learning capacity reaches full maturity, or comes very close to full maturity, within the first four or five years of life. (General intellectual capacity does not reach full maturity until considerably later, at about age eighteen.)

The fully mature capacity to acquire human language persists until the onset of puberty (at about age twelve). At that age the child's capacity to learn language diminishes abruptly. This diminution of language-learning capacity is evident in the difference between the second-language–learning capacities of children and of adults. A preadolescent child placed in continual contact with a foreign language will, within a matter of months, develop near-native pronunciation, fluency, and proficiency. A child whose first exposure to that same language comes in his late teens will learn it much more slowly, with obvious interference from his native language and a lingering trace of "foreign accent." There are as yet no adequate explanations for this abrupt diminution of language-learning capacity; nor is it clear how much of a person's natural language-learning capacity is in fact lost. The capacity to learn language does not completely disappear at puberty. Indeed, the capacity to increase vocabulary, to increase proficiency in formal speech, and to master new linguistic strategies obviously continues into adulthood, but the adult learner seems to lack the special talents of the child.

Given the sudden drop in language-learning capacity at about the age of most high-school freshmen, the traditional policy of postponing foreign-language teaching until high school or college seems woefully misguided. The preschool and elementary-school years are the period in which students are best able to use their natural language-learning capacities. High-school or college teachers must realize that their students will be entering the classroom less than fully capable of responding to teaching techniques based on natural language-learning capacities.

Both high-school and elementary-school teachers of language-related skills must recognize another limitation of natural language learning—namely, that reading and writing, unlike speaking and listening, do *not* come naturally. Speaking and understanding speech are the biological birthright of all children in all cultures, but some cultures have no written language and in cultures with a written language some children remain illiterate. Learning to read and write *requires* formal instruction. Children learning to read English, for instance, must be taught that the words on a page proceed from left to right. The alphabetical coding of words and sounds is also difficult for children to grasp without instruction. In learning to read and write, a child must master an unnatural manifestation of a natural language. The special problems of teaching him how to do so are discussed in later chapters of this book.

Five Principles of Natural Language Learning

Because language learning is natural to all children, teachers can predict their students' level of linguistic achievement; they can predict which language skills children will have mastered by the time they enter school, and which others they will master during their years in primary school and secondary school. But the fact that language learning is a natural phenomenon has still another important consequence for teachers. If a teacher is to aid his students in their natural acquisition of language skills, his teaching methods must encourage the natural language-learning tendencies operating within his students: he must not work against such tendencies. The most efficient teaching of language skills takes advantage of the natural language-learning talents students bring to the classroom. In order to take advantage of these talents, the teacher must understand how natural language learning operates—not simply *what* it accomplishes but *how* it accomplishes what it does. The following principles describe five general characteristics of language learning in school-age children.

Principle 1: The acquisition of each new language skill is a gradual process. The point at which a learner becomes able to use a new language feature (a new word, a new sentence structure, etc.) in his own speech is preceded by an extended time during which he indicates an emerging recognition of that language feature in the speech of others. More briefly, comprehension (an indication of passive mastery) precedes production (an indication of active mastery). The one-year-old child gives clear evidence of understanding, at least partially, the simple commands, statements, and questions he hears from adults. Yet a child that age has scarcely begun to produce language. It will be months or even years before he is able to produce sentences as complex as those he can understand at the age of one year. This principle explains the discrepancy frequently noted by educators between a child's passive vocabulary (the words he can understand) and his active vocabulary (the words he uses in his own speech): passive vocabulary is invariably much larger than active vocabulary. Many, but by no means all, of the words in a child's passive vocabulary will, at a later stage in his development, be produced actively.

Here is one example of how this principle can be used in the classroom. Assume that the teacher is presenting a vocabulary list which includes, among other words, the word *conspicuous*. The ultimate objective is that students learn how to use this word appropriately in an original sentence—that is, that they gain active mastery of the word. A pretest of the class tells the teacher that in fact they cannot now meet this objective. He then gives a further pretest to determine whether the students have at least reached the level of passive mastery. Such a test might present the students with a set of sentences containing the subject word. For example: (1) *Elgin Baylor, who is 6 feet 5 inches tall, would be more conspicuous on the street than among other players on a basketball court.* (2) *If you look conspicuous, the audience probably won't notice you.* And so on. The students would be asked to indicate which sentences were true and which were false. If they fail this second pretest as well, showing that they lack even a passive mastery of the word, then the teacher's first task is to instill this passive mastery by offering examples of the word used appropriately in a variety of contexts. If, on the other hand, the second pretest shows that the students have already mastered the word passively, they can be encouraged to move from this passive mastery to active mastery.

Principle 2: Children in the process of learning a language are mastering many language skills simultaneously. If, as principle 1 asserts, the complete mastery of each language skill is a gradual process requiring months or years, no language learner can afford the luxury of completely mastering one skill before tackling the next. Children do not master the pronunciation of vowels completely before moving on to consonants; they do not master the classification and subclassification of verbs before moving on to nouns or adjectives; they are simultaneously sorting out the set of inflections appropriate for verbs and the other sets appropriate for adjectives, nouns, and pronouns; almost from the beginning they are struggling to ask questions, make statements and demands, and to understand and respond to the questions, statements, and commands put to them by others. In any natural language-learning situation, children are forced to deal with all aspects of language at once. That is the way they receive language from other members of their speech community, and that is the way they learn it.

This method of learning by juggling several half-learned skills is difficult for some teachers to accept, perhaps because it so obviously does not apply to the learning of nonlanguage skills. Normally, the most efficient procedure for teaching a complex skill is to isolate its component skills and focus the learner's attention on each of them in turn, gradually adding more and more components. But this procedure does not seem to work well in language teaching—perhaps because the components of a language are not combined by addition but by a complex interaction in which one additional part changes the configuration of many of the existing parts. Learning a new word is not accomplished simply by understanding its meaning; frequently, the task also involves changing the scope of the meaning of other words. It is like adding one more piece to a puzzle that is already complete: existing pieces have to be altered or rearranged.

Typically, students are given a short list of new words to be learned within a week's time. Each student is expected to be able to pronounce every word properly and to use each word in an original sentence—that is, he is expected to have gained an *active* mastery of a small set of new words before beginning the task of learning additional new words. But instead of assigning a new small list of words each Monday to be mastered actively by the following Friday, teachers might experiment with vocabulary-development programs in which the words for an entire school year are systematically incorporated into the lecture and reading material for that year. Thus students would be given a longer passive exposure to a larger set of words. Only during the latter part of the school year would students be encouraged to demonstrate active mastery of the year's vocabulary.

Principle 3: Children learn how to speak with little if any conscious awareness of the nature of the language they are learning. In other words, they learn *how* without learning *about*. Even adult language-users have few conscious insights into what they are doing when they speak. They can label their own speech and the speech of others as appropriate or inappropriate, grammatical or ungrammatical, but they cannot explain the rules that enable them to apply these labels. Most language users simply do not know much *about* the grammatical system they employ. This fact seems to separate the use of language from all of the other intellectual skills that children learn in school. In teaching an intellectual skill the teacher usually encourages the student to understand the principles underlying his performance, and then to practice employing these principles in perfecting the skill. For example, in teaching the student how to find words in a dictionary, the teacher first encourages him to understand the ordering principles that govern the listing of words in the dictionary, and then to apply these principles in looking up particular words. Although this sequencing of learning tasks can be applied to most intellectual skills, natural language-learning principles suggest that it may *not* be appropriate in the mastery of language skills.

Principle 3 calls into question two widely held assumptions about language teaching. Many teachers assume that students must learn to define new words if they are to expand their vocabulary. Successfully incorporating a new word into one's vocabulary does not require the ability to define it, however. Knowing the definition of a word means knowing something about that word, not how to use it. In defining any English word the student must verbalize an equation relating that word to one or more other English words that are semantically equivalent to it. The ability to define a word is different from a knowledge of how to use it to convey meaning. Ask an elementary-school child to explain the meaning of some of the words he uses correctly and appropriately. The results should indicate that children almost always learn to use new words without being able to state their definitions.

Principle 3 also contradicts the assumption that learning about English grammar is an efficient means of increasing proficiency in writing compositions. If a student is having trouble expressing himself in writing, so the assumption goes, what he needs is a good dose of English grammar. But a course in English grammar is almost always a course *about* language. If knowing how neither presupposes nor requires knowing about, this cure for bad writing holds little promise of success.

Principle 4: Children learn to understand and use language by hearing it and later employing it themselves in situations that make the meaning clear. A child learns, for example, to use the word *cat* by hearing that word used appropriately in the presence of real or pictured cats. Although children, and for that matter adults, are not aware of the grammatical system they employ in their speech (see principle 3, above), they are clearly and consciously aware of the relationship between the words and sentences they use and the objects and situations outside language in the real world for which such words and sentences are appropriate.[2] Natural language learning occurs in a semantically appropriate nonlinguistic context. Such linguistic procedures as repeating lists of words or sentences without understanding and focusing attention on the meaning of these words and sentences represent unnatural language learning.

This principle is often difficult for teachers to utilize, for the range of experiences that can be produced or simulated in the classroom is limited. Language drills are easy to administer, but providing practice in using language in context is far more difficult. This difficulty is most obvious in foreign language classes. Although important advances have been made in the appropriateness of drill material—for instance, the old conjugation and declension drills (je suis, tu es, il est) have given way to drills that are more closely associated with language usage, such as substitution and transformation drills—students are still forced to manipulate the subject language outside the contexts in which it is appropriate. As they learn a foreign language, students still focus on language structure rather than on the association of structure with meaning.

Principle 5: In his own speech the language learner follows the linguistic norms of the individuals or groups with whom he identifies or wishes to identify. This is an area of language learning in which active language skills and passive language skills conform to different rules. Children learn to understand any and all individuals with whom they are in frequent contact—including those they know only by way of television or radio. This principle holds

---

[2] To say that speakers of a language are conscious of the association between words and sentences on the one hand and between objects and situations on the other is not to say that they are able to state in some general form the range of objects for which a particular noun is appropriate or the range of situations for which a given sentence is appropriate.

even when the language learner is exposed to a wide variety of different dialects or to many different languages. However, although the child learns to understand the speech of all those with whom he shares experiences, he does not draw upon these sources equally in formulating his own speech norms. He learns the ways of speaking that he feels are appropriate for the roles he chooses to assume: he learns the speech norms of the groups of which he perceives himself a member. And for the child growing up in the United States, that generally means his own age group. Teachers tend to overrate their importance as linguistic models for students. Most students do not want to sound like a teacher; they want to sound like other students. Teachers who constantly force adult speech norms on elementary-school or high-school students may inhibit rather than encourage the natural process whereby children come to view themselves as young adults and to adopt the speech norms appropriate for this new self-image. Perhaps the best counsel for teachers is to be patient and to encourage students to express themselves coherently and even beautifully without forcing them to sound like adults.

The punning in the title of this chapter is intentional: the chapter is about the learning of natural languages; it is also about natural as opposed to artificial or mechanical ways of teaching or learning a natural language. The metaphors traditionally associated with language learning in schools are mechanical. Children are taught to "construct" more complicated sentences or to "build" a larger vocabulary. But from the view of natural language learning presented here such metaphors seem inappropriate. Language is not constructed like an office building from blueprints spread out in the contractor's shack; rather, guided by the individual's internal blueprint, it grows more like a tree whose every living cell determines the way in which it will be nourished and shaped by its environment. And if languages develop more like trees than like buildings, language teachers should be more like gardeners than like mechanics. Their job is to recognize and create environments in which the potential for language growth, present within all human beings, can be most fully and magnificently realized.

THE LINGUISTICS OF READING

Learning to read is related to but different from natural language learning; some of the skills necessary for reading have little or nothing to do with language. The reader must learn, for example, to move his eyes across the page from left to right and then down the page to the next line, to make these eye movements with appropriate spacing and duration, and to recognize the visual differences that distinguish the letters of the alphabet while ignoring stylistic differences in the printing or writing of the same letter; such skills are only remotely associated with language. But reading also requires the capacity to associate written symbols with a pre-existing language system or code (what linguists call *language competence* or *internalized grammar*) and to understand those symbols in terms of that code. This capacity links reading with natural language skills.

Anyone able to assign meaning to language sounds and, conversely, to express meaning through language sounds must have mastered some coding system that relates sound and meaning.

---

language sounds ⟵——— **(coding system)** ———⟶ **meaning**

For English and for all other natural human languages, the coding system has an intermediate stage at which the language is represented as a sequence of words. Linguists call this intermediate stage the *surface structure*.

---

language sounds ← (subcode) → sequence of words (surface structure) ← (subcode) → meaning

---

Language sounds, then, are associated by one subcoding system with a sequence of words, and this sequence of words is associated by another subcoding system with meaning.

Two further statements must be made regarding this simplified model of a language coding system. First, the language user frequently perceives words as composed of meaningful subparts. Linguists call these smallest meaningful units *morphemes* (see Chapter 2, p. 19). The word *walked* contains two morphemes: one meaning a form of human or animal locomotion, the other meaning past tense. Second, at this intermediate stage of the language code, the language user perceives a sequence of words arranged as phrases which in turn form parts of larger phrases. So, for example, the sentence *The dish ran away with the spoon* has as its surface structure first the sequence of morphemes: *the-dish-run+past-away-with-the-spoon*. In addition, this sequence is arranged in a hierarchy of phrases: *the-dish* form one phrase as do *run+past* and *the-spoon*. *Run+past* combines with *away* to form the larger phrase *run+past-away*. Similarly, the word *with* combines with the phrase *the-spoon* to form a larger phrase, which in turn combines with *run+past-away* to form the complete verb phrase. Finally, the verb phrase combines with the first noun phrase, *the-dish*, to form the complete sentence. The following "tree diagram" represents this hierarchy of phrases:

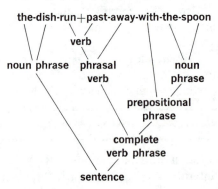

Thus the language code can be represented in a more complete form as:

---

language sounds	← (subcode) →	sequence of morphemes arranged in phrasal hierarchy (surface structure)	← (subcode) →	meaning

---

The intermediate (surface-structure) stage of the language code is particularly important for a reader of English because the written symbols for English represent not only language sounds but also various characteristics of the surface structure.[1]

In English, the visual symbols are associated with the language code in at least four different ways. First, the temporal sequence of words or morphemes in the surface structure of an English sentence is represented as a linear (left-to-right, top-to-bottom) sequence of spaced groups of letters. Second, each individual word or morpheme is represented by a particular sequence of letters which is repeated each time that word or morpheme occurs. Third, within each written word or morpheme, individual letters or combinations of letters stand for individual units of sound in pronunciation. As was the case with the linear sequencing of words, the linear sequence of letters within words represents the temporal sequence of sounds in the pronunciation of those words. Finally, the various punctuation marks used in writing English represent divisions of the phrasal hierarchy of the surface structure. Commas mark the boundary of certain types of phrases, and periods and capital letters mark the boundaries of sentences.

[1] The precise form of the association between written symbols and the language code varies from language to language. For some languages the association is mainly between written symbols and sounds; the other written symbols of other languages, such as the characters used to represent Chinese, stand for individual words or morphemes but contain no information as to how those words or morphemes should be pronounced—just as the arabic numerals (1, 2, 3, etc.) similarly contain no phonic information about the English words they are used to symbolize. Because of the differences among languages in what written symbols represent, the skills that must be learned in order to read one language are not necessarily identical with the skills needed to read another language. In this chapter the focus is on the range of skills required for reading English.

If the bond between written English and the English language code were as regular and precise as this series of correspondences suggests, learning how to read English would be an easier task than it in fact is. Unfortunately, however, none of the correspondences outlined above is without exception or limitation.

Only the first correspondence, between temporal sequencing of words and linear ordering, is almost without exception; written English usually moves from left to right within a line and from the top to bottom between successive lines. But in rare instances—such as around the edge of coins

and on traffic signs

—even this first correspondence is violated. The second and third correspondences are far less precise, and in some cases they are even incompatible. The spelling of a single word or morpheme is always the same, according to the second correspondence. At the same time, according to the third correspondence, that spelling always represents the pronunciation of the particular word or morpheme. These two correspondences work together consistently only when every speaker of English always pronounces the given word or morpheme in exactly the same way. But, of course, such instances are rare: different people under different circumstances pronounce almost any given word in different ways. In most cases, therefore, either the consistent representation of morphemes and words (correspondence 2) or the consistent representation of pronunciation (correspondence 3) must yield to the facts of English pronunciation. Even beyond this inherent incompatibility English spelling is full of annoying inconsistencies. Occasionally, the same word can be spelled more than one way (*traveled/travelled*; *advertise/advertize*). Much more frequently, one spelling can stand for two different words. Such identical spellings may even occur when the words are pronounced differently (*read* = [rid] and [rɛd]; *bow* = [bo] and [baw]).[2] The correspondence in English between letters of the alphabet and individual sounds is notoriously bad. The same English sound can be represented by a number of different letters of the alphabet. Conversely, a single letter of the alphabet can represent a number of different English sounds. The fourth correspondence, between English punctuation and the boundaries of phrases and sentences, also has a number of inconsistencies. The rules for punctuating English sentences differ somewhat from one author or from one publisher to another. Moreover, none of these rules provides complete information about phrase boundaries in English sentences. English punctuation does not, for example, indicate the important phrase boundary between the subject and the predicate of a sentence.

Because the correspondence between written English and the English language code is imperfect, reading English cannot be simply a matter of memorizing and applying mechanically a set of correspondence rules. All such rules are bound to have exceptions, and keeping the rules and the exceptions straight requires more intellectual prowess than most beginning readers are able to muster. Those who succeed in learning to read English master a number of alternative strategies for figuring out what English words, phrases, and sentences form a given written passage. Their degree of success at reading depends on their ability to employ these different strategies simultaneously, rapidly, and accurately in making judgments about how written symbols relate to the English language code. Helping children learn how to read involves helping them to master these different reading strategies. It is important, therefore, that teachers know, first, what these strategies are and, second, how to recognize whether their students are employing or failing to employ each strategy. Consequently the remainder of this chapter describes a number of reading strategies and suggests some ways in which a teacher can recognize their development in a student's reading.

---

[2] The sounds associated with the phonetic symbols used here and elsewhere in this chapter are explained in the chapter appendix, "Key to Pronunciation."

Reading Strategy 1:
Whole-Word/Morpheme Recognition

The reader following this strategy learns to associate the shape or configuration of the written representation of a word with the word itself. He sees the word as a whole, then says it—without considering each letter individually or looking within the word for clues as to the sounds it contains. He views the word in much the same way that all readers view an arabic numeral: as a unit without internal phonic clues.

Whole-word recognition has a number of advantages. Since the reader does not first have to learn a system of phonetic values for the letters composing words, this strategy is easy to teach; it is often taught to students at the very beginning of their training in reading. They are encouraged to begin reading by learning how to recognize at sight a basic set of frequently occurring English words. Those words that a child learns to recognize as whole units are referred to as his *sight vocabulary*. Besides being simple to teach, the whole-word recognition strategy enables the learner to read rapidly and fluently: the recognition of words is instantaneous. Because speed-reading complex material requires this sort of instantaneous word recognition, skilled adult readers also rely heavily on the strategy of whole-word recognition. Indeed an extensive recognition vocabulary is one of the marks of a proficient adult reader.

But teachers would be seriously in error if they attempted to teach reading solely by means of the whole-word recognition strategy, for it has some serious disadvantages which must be corrected by additional strategies. A reader relying solely on whole-word recognition would be able to read only those words he had previously been taught. Such a reader would lack what reading teachers call "word attack skills." Moreover, whole-word recognition strategy strains the visual and perceptual memory of the reader. The more words in a child's sight vocabulary, the greater the chance that he will confuse two words which are visually or semantically similar. A child limited to whole-word recognition strategy may see the word *the* and read "one," or he may see the word *lion* and read "tiger." Such mistakes would not be made by a child able to support his guess with phonic evidence. Whole-word recognition strategy also becomes more difficult to apply as the beginning reader encounters more and more different styles and sizes of type. His recognition, then, can no longer be purely visual. He must be able to generalize a single word from the various upper- and lower-case type faces that he encounters in reading.

The strategy of morpheme recognition is closely allied to word recognition; but in morpheme recognition the learner is encouraged to recognize recurring morpheme units within words. For example, the reader seeing the word *helping* would be trained to perceive this word as containing two morpheme units: *help* and *-ing*. This strategy is a useful addition to whole-word recognition because it does provide the reader with some basis for recognizing new words. A morpheme-recognition reader who has learned to read the words *helping* and *played* should also be able to read the words *helped* and *playing*.

Reading Strategy 2:
Sounding Out Words by Letter

This is the strategy frequently referred to by teachers as the phonic approach. Following this strategy, the reader associates a sound with each of the letters in a word and then arrives at the whole word by combining the individual sounds. This would be an extremely effective strategy if there were a one-to-one correspondence between the letters of the English alphabet and the sounds of English. In a spelling system ideal for this strategy every letter of the alphabet represents one and only one sound, and every sound is represented by one and only one letter of the alphabet. Unfortunately, English spelling deviates from one-to-one letter-to-sound correspondence in four different ways. First, one letter may represent a sequence of two sounds. For example, the letter *x* represents the sequence of sounds [ks] (as in *tax*).[3] Second, a sequence of two letters may represent a single sound. Such a combination of letters (for instance, *th* or *ph*) is frequently called a *diagraph*. Third, the same sound may be spelled in two or more different ways. For example, the English sound [k] may be spelled, among

---

[3] In addition, the letter *x* can represent the sequence [gz] as in *exaggerate*. Thus, the letter *x* is an example not only of irregular type 1 but of type 4 as well.

other ways, either as the letter *c* or as the letter *k*. Fourth, a single letter of the alphabet or a sequence of two letters may stand for two or more different sounds. Consider, for example, the sounds associated with the letter *s* in the words *song, confusion,* and *busy*.

The following chart illustrates these four irregular types of spelling-sound correspondence:

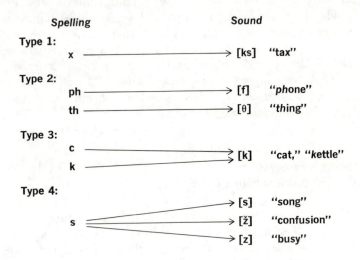

The arrows in this chart represent the mental paths followed by the reader in associating printed symbols with English sounds.

These four types of deviation from one letter–one sound correspondence should be recognized individually, since each one prompts a different set of problems for the reader. Most readers seem able to learn types 1 and 2 without difficulty. Type 3 adds to the amount of learning needed to read but does not make that learning more complex. When the same sound can be spelled two ways, the reader is simply required to learn two different equations involving that sound. Spelling-sound mismatches of type 3 decrease the efficiency of the spelling system but do not drastically increase its difficulty for the reader. Type 4, on the other hand, presents serious problems for the reader trying to sound out words. Like type 3, it demands that the reader learn two or more equations or correspondences. Faced with the type 4 example in the preceding chart, for instance, the reader would have to master three correspondences involving the letter *s* and learn to associate it with the sounds [s], [ž], and [z]. However, knowing this triple correspondence would not itself enable the reader to sound out new words. Presented with the letter *s* in a new word he would still have to figure out which of the three possible correspondences is correct for that particular word. Should he sound out the word as containing the sound [s] or [ž] or [z]? This kind of additional question does not arise for any of the three other types of irregular correspondence. In answering it, the reader may follow one of two approaches: either he may employ a trial-and-error strategy using first one sound and then, if necessary, another; or he may learn some additional rules that will tell him which of the two sounds is likely to be correct in this particular word. For example, he might learn that in English when the letter *s* is at the beginning of a word and is followed by some letter other than *h*, it is pronounced with the sound [s]; that the letter *s* in the word-final sequence *-sion* is pronounced [ž]; and that the letter *s* appearing elsewhere in the middle of words and surrounded there by vowels is frequently pronounced [z].

These rules tend to be complicated, but trial-and-error guessing can be even more complicated, especially when more than one type 4 spelling-sound correspondence occurs in the same word. If a word contains two multisound symbols, then it has at least four possible pronunciations; if there are three, at least eight pronunciations are possible. In the example above, the letter *s* was shown to represent at least three different sounds in English. If this letter is only one of several multisound symbols in a particular word, the pronunciation possibilities become even more unwieldy.

The preceding discussion of irregular spelling-sound correspondence in English has maintained the fiction that they are clearly separable, each affecting different letters of the alphabet. In fact, however, most letters of the English alphabet are irregular in several different ways. The following chart provides a more realistic view of the confusion of English spelling by focusing on the letters *s, c,* and *k* as they are used in English spelling. It does not, however, exhaust the possible uses of these three letters in English, since the sequences *ch, sh, sch,* for example, are not included. But even within its small fragment of the English spelling system, the chart provides three examples of irregular correspondence type 2, two examples of type 3, and three examples of type 4.

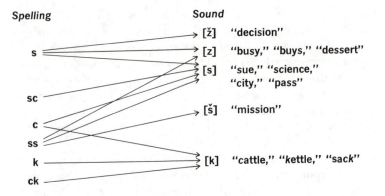

Sounding out words letter by letter is the ultimate strategy in word attack; its advantages in reading English are obvious. But as earlier paragraphs have discussed, the language's lack of a rigid one-to-one correspondence between letters and sounds and its frequent type 4 correspondences make this strategy an extremely complex one for readers to apply. Even if a one-to-one letter-sound correspondence predominated, sounding out words letter by letter would still have the serious disadvantage of being an extremely slow process. The fluent reader cannot afford the time required to sound out each word he reads, only an occasional new word. Those students who seem to sound out most or many of the words they encounter are generally at an early stage in their reading development.

Reading Strategy 3:
Sounding Out Words by Multiple-Letter Units

It is also possible to sound out words by considering groups of letters and learning to associate a set of sounds with a sequence of letters. The words *cat, hat,* and *sat,* for instance, each have the same last two letters, which form a sequence that is pronounced the same way in each word. A reader might sound out any of these words by learning the sound of the initial consonant and combining this sound with the ones associated with the sequence of letters *at*. In the case of three-letter words like *cat*, this procedure seems to have no advantage over sounding out words letter by letter; but in sounding out more complicated words, the reader would find it advantageous to consider a sequence of letters as a unit. The sequence *-tion* at the end of English words is almost always pronounced the same way,[4] and yet this pronunciation is not a combination of the sounds normally associated with the individual letters. The sequence of letters *oo* is generally pronounced in one of two ways in English: with a short vowel as in the word *book* or with a long vowel as in the word *cool*. If the reader is taught to sound out this double-vowel sequence by itself, each time he encounters it he must somehow decide which of these two sounds he will use. If, on the other hand, he learns to sound out *oo* in conjunction with a following consonant, a trial-and-error choice will seldom be necessary: the pronunciation of this double vowel can usually be predicted on the basis of the subsequent consonant. When the following consonant is *l*, for example, or when there is no following consonant, the *oo* sequence is regularly pronounced as a long vowel; but when the *oo* is followed by *k*, it is (except in the word *kook*) pronounced as a short vowel. Given this patterned alternation of pronunciation, it seems worthwhile that in sounding out words the reader be encouraged to consider the sequences *ool* and *ook* as units.

Sounding out words by larger-than-single-letter units provides one alternative to endless trial-and-error guessing or the memorization of vast numbers of complex letter-sound correspondence rules. It is particularly applicable when the spelling system contains recurring sequences that are phonetically irregular, or when the pronunciation of one letter can be regularly predicted from the presence of some neighboring letter.

This reading strategy is useful, however, only as a supplement to strategies for sounding out words by letter. It is not a self-sufficient approach to reading, since the reader sounding out words will almost always encounter stray single letters along with multiletter sequences. Furthermore, since this strategy works by encouraging the reader to recognize and use recurring sequences of letters, it is useful only when the reader has mastered enough

---

[4] That is, *-tion* is normally pronounced [šən] as in *nation*. Words such as *equation* and *question* contain exceptions to this generalization—but the words *exception* and *generalization* do not.

words to be able to do so. This strategy is useful for the beginning reader only if the vocabulary of his reading texts is selected to make recurring patterns apparent. Teachers who have used such texts may recognize the "fat-cat-sat-on-the-mat" approach. Finally, relying primarily on multiletter sequences drastically increases the number of letter-sound correspondences to be mastered. English uses only twenty-six letters, but these twenty-six letters form many times that many two- or three-letter sequences. In fact, as these sequences increase in length, their number approaches the number of English words, and multiletter strategy becomes more like whole-word recognition strategy.

Reading Strategy 4:
Associating Spelling with Underlying Phonological Form

Morphemes and words in English often change in pronunciation when combined with some other morpheme. For example, the last consonant sound of the word *Paris* changes when the suffix *-ian* is added; the same change occurs when the suffix *-ion* is added to the word *revise*. While in both these cases the final consonant sound changes, its spelling remains unchanged. Most teachers would consider this just one more example of the frustrating lack of correspondence between English spelling and English pronunciation, but often such changes in pronunciation are governed by some fairly general and consistent rules.[5] For example, one such rule states that when vowels in English become totally unstressed, they all tend to be pronounced the same way: with the vowel sound called *schwa* [ə], which appears at the end of words like *sofa* and *soda*. This "rule"—reducing vowel sounds to schwa when these vowels become unstressed—is followed consistently but unconsciously by all speakers of English. Speakers of English know how each syllable of an English word would be pronounced if it

---

[5] By far the most ambitious and important attempt to state these rules for English is Noam Chomsky and Morris Halle, *The Sound Pattern of English* (New York: Harper and Row, 1968). Chomsky and Halle also suggest (pp. 49–50) that the consistent correspondence they observe between underlying phonological form and English spelling would provide a basis for teaching reading to speakers of English.

were fully stressed; in addition they know which syllables are in fact stressed in each occurrence of the word or morpheme; and finally, they know the rule described above for changing the sound of vowels in the unstressed syllables.

What makes this fact about English pronunciation important in the present discussion is that some English spellings that seem to be very irregular and inconsistent representations of the way English words or morphemes are pronounced turn out to be regular and consistent representations of the sounds of these same words or morphemes before rules like the one on vowel reduction are applied. Words are often spelled as if every syllable were pronounced with full stress. Consider the pronunciation of the underlined vowels in each of the following pairs of words:

combíne—cómbinátion

Japán—Jápanése

démocrátic—demócracy

The words in each pair contain the same morpheme, but each one stresses different syllables of that morpheme. Note that in all cases the spelling of the vowels is an imperfect representation of the actual pronunciation of those words because the vowels in the unstressed syllables are pronounced with a schwa; however, the spelling is perfectly regular for the stressed syllables. These spellings, then, make very good sense as long as we know which syllables are stressed and what happens to the sound of unstressed vowels.

Some linguists have argued that children learning how to read can be taught to view spelling as representing not the pronunciation of words but rather the phonological form underlying the pronunciation of words prior to the application of rules like the stress-reduction rule. If the reader perceived the printed form of words and morphemes in this way, then sounding out words would involve applying such rules to the form of the word given in the spelling.

This approach to sounding out words has at least one important advantage: English spelling, so notoriously irregular when considered as representing actual pronunciation, becomes much more regular when taken as a representation of the abstract phonological form of words prior to the application of the various phonological rules. Theoretically, instead of dealing with a system of spelling riddled with annoying exceptions, the child who associates spelling with underlying phonological form could learn sounding-out rules that have fewer exceptions and more predictive power.

But the usefulness of this strategy depends on the young reader's capacity to perceive and use a knowledge of underlying phonological forms. Unless the reader is consciously aware of these forms and aware of their relationship to the actual pronunciation of English, he will not be able to use them to relate spoken and written English.[6] So far, no clear evidence exists that this association between underlying phonological representation and pronunciation can be made conscious to the degree necessary for its use as a reading strategy. Moreover, it may not be reasonable to expect that children just past school age will have learned underlying phonological forms; perhaps these forms are mastered only by older children and adults. Most of the changes in stress and in the other crucial aspects of the pronunciation of a single English morpheme occur in the learned, Latinate vocabulary of English rather than in the more basic Anglo-Saxon words that predominate in the vocabulary of children. Finally, even if the underlying phonological forms do somehow exist in the English-speaking child's subconscious linguistic knowledge, and even if these forms could somehow be brought to consciousness, there is no assurance that the child would be able to relate these forms to the written representation of morphemes. For these reasons, this reading strategy must be considered at best an interesting suggestion which may at some time in the future join the list of strategies that reading teachers can equip their students to use.

[6] A proposal for encouraging students to sound out or recognize words based on their knowledge of the underlying phonological form of those words raises an even more fundamental linguistic issue. Clearly, the system of phonological rules that Chomsky and Halle (see footnote 5) describe does with convincing regularity arrive at the various pronunciations of English morphemes. That is, the end product of the rules is an observably accurate representation of the pronunciation of English. It is not equally clear, however, that the system of rules (which includes the concept of underlying phonological form) corresponds in some clear and direct way to the psychological processes involved in speech production. The association between such psychological processes and the system of formally stated linguistic rules may be comparable to the association between a trombone and an electronic gadget capable of producing all of the sounds of a trombone. The end result of both these sound-producing systems would be the same, but the internal mechanisms leading to that end result would be quite different.

Reading Strategy 5:
Feedback and Anticipation Strategies

In all of the strategies mentioned so far, the student-reader must use imperfect evidence to figure out what word is confronting him on the printed page; and therefore this process involves considerable guesswork. Fortunately, readers who know the language they are reading have three sorts of feedback that help them decide whether to accept some particular guess or to reject it as incorrect or improbable.

First, when a reader knows the language he is reading, he will try to make each of the words he reads correspond to a word he recognizes as part of the language. In sounding out a written word, he will reject as incorrect all of the guesses that result in a sequence of noises he does not know to be a spoken word in his language; and he will tend to accept any sequence of noises he does recognize as a spoken word. Given the sequence of letters *b-o-o-k*, for instance, he will reject "bowk" [bok] and "buke" [buk], but he will almost certainly accept "book" [buk].

A second form of feedback applies when the reader is aware of the grammatical context in which the word he is reading appears. If the word he sounds out is grammatically appropriate for that context, then he will tend to accept it; if it is grammatically inappropriate, he will reject it. Thus, for example, if the reader encounters the sentence *The XXXXX waddled slowly*, he will know that the unidentified sequence of letters represents a *noun*. He is not necessarily aware of the term *noun*, but he has, as part of the process of language learning, classified the words in his language into categories one of which corresponds to what linguists and teachers call *nouns*. The child-reader knows that the word he must sound out will fall within that category of words. If this sounding out produces a word which is not in that category, even if the word is recognizably English, the reader employing this feedback strategy will reject it and try again.

The reader employs a third feedback strategy when he uses appropriateness of meaning as a basis for accepting or rejecting some guess that he has made in sounding out words. The reader in the preceding paragraph, for example, might sound out the word *people* to complete the sentence *The XXXXX waddled slowly*. He might decide, however, that *people* does not make sense here, since generally people are not supposed to waddle. He might therefore again try to sound out the word and arrive this time at the word *penguin*. The feedback he receives from meaning would now be more positive: penguins do literally waddle. This guess would be semantically appropriate and therefore confirmed by the third form of feedback.

Just as a knowledge of words, of grammar, and of semantic appropriateness provides feedback for the reader, it also enables readers to anticipate what the next word is going to be. Even without looking at a word, a reader can often predict it based on his understanding of what the preceding portions of the sentence or passage are saying. Many of the "mistakes" made by experienced readers are anticipations of this sort that turn out to be incorrect. But such guesses and such feedback are only available to the reader who understands the language of the passage he is reading. If the reader does not understand the language, then all the noises he makes in sounding out words will seem equally strange to him; none will cause him to try again rather than read on. Similarly, if the grammatical structure is strange—because the material is in a foreign language, a foreign dialect of the reader's language, or merely an unfamiliar style of his own dialect—the reader may get negative feedback even when he has read the right word. And, of course, if the reader does not understand the meaning of what he is reading, because he is unfamiliar, for example, with the subject matter or with the language, then the third form of feedback is impossible. If a reader of the sentence about penguins waddling slowly does not know anything about penguins, he will not know that they were likely candidates for the subject of the verb *waddle*.

In order to use feedback and anticipation strategies, the student must be able to separate learning how to read from learning the skills necessary to employ feedback strategies—that is, from learning new vocabulary, new styles of English, new dialects of English, new information. Too often teachers use the reading assignment to teach new vocabulary or new facts and information, or to encourage a student to pronounce words according to a different set of dialectal or stylistic norms than he presently follows; occasionally reading is used to teach an entirely new language. In all these cases, because the language itself is in some way unexpected or unfamiliar, the child is going to have a harder time recognizing the association between the printed form of language and the language system that he already knows. Reading instruction, certainly at its beginning stages and for children who are having unusual difficulty, should use only those sentence structures, words, dialects, styles, and topics with which the reader is already familiar.

Children also have more difficulty reading words that appear in isolation as part of a list than they have reading those that are part of a sentence. When words appear in isolation, neither the second nor the third form of feedback can be employed. Consequently, in teaching word recognition, a teacher should try to present new words in sentences; and only after the class has learned to recognize these words in context should they be presented for identification in isolation, apart from any semantic or grammatical context.

An Analysis of Reading Strategies

A student learning to read should be taught to employ a full range of strategies for deciphering written English. But a teacher may have difficulty determining his success in teaching different reading strategies since standard reading achievement tests do not isolate reading strategies. Because the kinds of errors a student makes in oral reading depend on the types of strategies he is employing, a teacher can use a student's oral reading errors as an indicator of that student's mastery of reading strategies.

The following analysis was made from a recording of Jeff, an eight-year-old third-grader, reading a fifteen-line passage. In this reading Jeff was left on his own without adult correction. The passage is presented here with the line divisions of the original retained and with the individual lines numbered.[7]

1. Father said, "I want to live where there are trees
2. so we can build a log cabin. A home with-
3. out trees around would never seem right."
4. And Timothy was glad they did have trees

---

[7] This passage appears in Glenn McCracken and Charles C. Walcutt, *Basic Reading* (Philadelphia: J. B. Lippincott Company, 1964), p. 157, and is reprinted here by permission of the publisher.

5. nearby as he thought of how good the wal-
6. nuts were going to taste in the turkey
7. stuffing.
8.   It was a long way to the walnut trees, so
9. Timothy had taken along slabs of cold corn-
10. bread, sweetened with wild honey, for a
11. lunch. As he walked along now, he felt a
12. crisp, cool breeze against his cheeks. The
13. autumn sky seemed bluer than in spring,
14. and the trees blazed with gaudy shades of
15. red and yellow.

The errors Jeff made in reading this passage are represented in the following table:

Line	Word or phrase	Error
2–3	with/out	"with (p)* out (p) without"
3	would never seem	"would be" (corrected self)
4	did have	"did not (p) have"
5	thought of how good	"thought how good"
5–6	how good the walnuts	"how good a walnuts (p) how good walnuts"
6	were going	(repeated)
9	slabs	(sounded out correctly)
10	sweetened	"[swit] (p) [switənd] (p) [swit] (p) [switɪnd] (reads on) [switənd]"
11	felt	"left"
12	crisp	"[kræšp] (p) [sræ] (p) [srɪsp] (p) [krɪsp]"
12	his	"the"
12	The	"he"
13	autumn	"[ən] (p) [təm] (p) [ɪn] (p) [atʊm]" (adult listener: "That's right") "[ɔdm̩]"
13	seemed	"[s:] (p) [simd]"
14	blazed	"[ble] (p) [blɪzd] (p) [blæzed] (p) [blæzd]"
14	gaudy	"[gl] (p) [glæ] (p) [glædi]"

* The symbol (p) indicates a pause in the reading.

At the end of line 2 and the beginning of line 3, the morphemes *with* and *out* were first read as two words with a clear break between them. They were immediately repeated as a single word without a break and with stronger stress on the second syllable. Although Jeff recognized the two morpheme components of the word in his first reading, it was only after he had finished reading them that he realized these two morphemes (separated visually by the length of a line and connected by the end-of-line hyphen) formed a single word. As a consequence he corrected his reading. This correction came as a result of feedback produced by a recognition of the word and perhaps also by a recognition of its appropriateness for the grammatical and semantic context.

In line 3 Jeff first read "A home without trees around would be . . ." but immediately corrected himself to "would never seem right." This error is possible only if the reader recognizes the meaning and the grammatical structure of what he is reading. Jeff anticipated the word *be* as a grammatically and semantically appropriate continuation of the sentence. When he looked at the actual word and saw that it was the word *never*, he recognized that his anticipated guess was wrong and changed the reading accordingly.

In line 4, the word *not* was inserted erroneously between the words *did* and *have*. Although Jeff paused over his error, he did not correct it. Perhaps Jeff found the meaning of this sentence confusing: if the trees were used to build a log cabin (as envisaged in line 2), they should no longer exist as trees; this confusion may have been reinforced by the phrase "a home without trees" in the preceding sentence. Furthermore, Jeff may have had difficulty because the use of the auxiliary verb *did* with special stress preceding a main verb as a means of emphasizing that verb does not occur in his dialect.[8] If Jeff wanted to compose a sentence using the emphatic sense of the word *did*, he would include the word *so* ("They did *so* have trees"); the sequence *they did have trees* is foreign to his dialect. Jeff's mistake suggests that he was translating what he was reading into the dialect he would ordinarily use in speaking. But such translation is only possible when the reader understands, at least in part, the meaning and grammatical structure of the reading passage. This is not, in other words, a beginner's mistake, for it implies a somewhat sophisticated mastery of reading skills.

[8] The word *dialect* is used here rather loosely to refer to speech norms within Jeff's small group of peers.

The next mistake, the omission of the word *of* in line 5, is again caused by a difference between the dialect of the reader and the dialect of the writer of the passage. For Jeff, the expression "thought how good" is more common than "thought of how good"; so he again reworded what he saw into his own dialect.

In line 5, the word *the* was read as "a." Words like the articles *the* and *a* are generally part of the initial sight vocabulary taught to beginning readers in the first and second grades. Because children are not encouraged at that stage to consider the phonological clues in words, they frequently confuse grammatically or semantically similar words even though these words are spelled and pronounced quite differently. Because of the grammatical similarity between *a* and *the*, they are likely to be confused. Coming to the word *walnuts* and noting the pluralizing -s in this word, Jeff realized that his initial reading of the indefinite article *a* could not be right because that article precedes only singular nouns. So Jeff left out the article altogether, assuming the passage should read: "he thought how good walnuts were going to taste." This reading, though still not what appears on the printed page, does make both grammatical and semantic sense. And because Jeff was responding to grammatical and semantic feedback, he was satisfied with this approximation.

In line 6, the words *were going* were read twice. This seems at first a surprising sort of correction since the words were correct the first time through. Yet Jeff, as a speaker of English, was indeed correcting himself. The sequence *were going* can mean two different things, depending on whether the word *going* is taken to represent the main verb or a part of the auxiliary element signifying future time. These two different meanings of *going* are represented in the two sentences *The child is going to school* and *The child is going to cry*. Only in the second of these sentences can the sequence *going to* be pronounced "gonna." No speaker of English, regardless of age, would say "the child is gonna school." At first, Jeff assumed that *going* was a main verb; but when he noted the infinitive phrase *to taste* after it, he realized that it was in fact an auxiliary element indicating future time. So he reread it, this time changing not what he said but how he perceived what he said. This kind of error is again possible only when the reader is a speaker of English receiving feedback from his recognition of English words (in this case English homonyms) and his awareness of how these words join in grammatically and semantically appropriate ways to form sentences.

In line 9, Jeff sounded out the word *slabs* without difficulty. Although he was unfamiliar with the written form of this word and needed to consider some phonic clues to its identity, his immediate acceptance of the results of his sounding out suggests that the word was familiar to him as part of his recognition vocabulary. Jeff selected the appropriate vowel on his first try: the short *a*, [æ]. This seems to suggest at least a partial mastery of the complex association between vowel letters and English vowel sounds. (However, in subsequent attempts to sound out words, Jeff indicated that perhaps he uses this short *a* as a first reading for a number of different vowel letters. For example, he used it in trying to sound out the vowel *i* in *crisp*, the long *a* vowel [ey] in *blazed*, and the digraph *au* [ɔ] in *gaudy*.) Once past the vowel sound, Jeff readily accepted the final *-s* in the word *slabs* as a marker of the plural. Without hesitation he applied the rules for pronouncing English plurals and correctly pronounced the *-s* in this case as a voiced sound—that is, a sound produced with the vocal cords vibrating.[9]

A more complex problem arose when Jeff encountered the word *sweetened*. He sounded out the word correctly, then rejected this pronunciation and tried to sound out the word again. Eventually he gave up and read on. When he completed the phrase *sweetened with wild honey*, he immediately repeated it with more confidence than at first and with the word *sweetened* now clearly accepted as correct. Jeff probably assumed in the initial reading that following the first comma in line 10 he would read the next item in a list of things that Timothy had taken along with him. Consequently, Jeff expected this word to be a noun rather than a past participle beginning a phrase that modified the preceding noun. Because he had anticipated the wrong kind of grammatical structure, he was puzzled and rejected his own correct reading. Only after he read past *sweetened* and discovered that indeed this word made good grammatical and semantic sense in the context did he reread and confirm his initial reading. This mistake again indicates anticipation of grammatical content and grammatical structure.

In line 11, the word *felt* was misread "left." Probably this switch-

[9] In English the plural marker *-s* is pronounced as a voiced sibilant when it follows a voiced sound other than /z/ /ž/ or /ǰ/.

ing of the letters *f* and *l* was caused by a visual confusion between sight-vocabulary words. This mistake had serious consequences in the next line when Jeff confronted the word *crisp,* which he did not recognize. Having confused *felt* and *left,* he had lost the possibility that semantic or grammatical feedback would help him read *crisp* properly and had to rely entirely on phonic clues in its spelling. His first attempt at sounding out the word was close, except that he got the vowel wrong and the *s* slightly wrong. The result was nonsense—certainly not a word that Jeff recognized. So he tried again, assuming erroneously that his mistake must have been an incorrect pronunciation of the initial letter *c.* He had first pronounced it as "k," so now he replaced the "k" with an "s." Since this too was clearly not an English word, he looked further and discovered his mistakes with the vowel and the *s;* these he corrected in his third attempt. Finally, in his fourth attempt he returned to his initial assumption that the letter *c* must be pronounced "k." He immediately accepted the reading [krɪsp] as correct and went on.

But Jeff was still not free of trouble, for he was still not sure about the meaning of what he was reading. Throughout line 12, he was hesitating, reading one word at a time, and making further mistakes. The two mistakes were substitutions of sight vocabulary: instead of the word *his* he read the word *the,* and instead of the word *the* he read the word *he,* perhaps responding in each case to the visual similarity between the two words.

Moving on to line 13, he encountered, again at the beginning of the line, a word that he did not recognize. But this time he had made enough uncorrected mistakes in the preceding line so that he was totally lost. His first reaction after looking at the word *autumn* was to groan, but then he tried to sound it out. At first he assumed that the initial *u* was an *n,* making a perceptual error common among new readers: namely, turning a letter upside down. Eventually one of his guesses approached the correct pronunciation of *autumn,* and this guess was confirmed by an adult listener. Following this confirmation, Jeff repeated the word *autumn,* this time pronouncing it as he normally would. Then he moved on through the line, though still unsure about the meaning of what he was reading. His insecurity was reflected in his hesitation over a word that he clearly knew, the word *seemed.* In line 3 he had read the word *seem* without difficulty.

In line 14, he encountered the word *blazed*. This relatively un-common word used here in a figurative rather than a literal sense was apparently meaningless to Jeff. His attempt to sound it out indicated the same confusion between the spelling of the sounds [æ] and [ɪ] that he had exhibited in his attempts to sound out the word *crisp*, and also suggested his ignorance of the rule distinguish-ing long and short pronunciations of the vowel *a*.[10]

Jeff failed in sounding out this word and failed even more miserably when he came to the word *gaudy* (again, a word almost certainly not a part of his speaking vocabulary). His final attempt at it was a vague approximation incorporating the initial *g* and final *-dy*.

Toward the end of this passage, Jeff lost touch with the semantic and grammatical context and consequently was unable to use the feedback mechanisms he had employed earlier in the reading. Even during his unsuccessful struggles with *blazed* and *gaudy*, how-ever, Jeff recognized that the final *-ed* of *blazed* and perhaps also the final *-y* of *gaudy* represented separate morphemes—the past tense morpheme and an adjective-formation morpheme. In both cases he had no difficulty sounding out these morpheme units. The *-ed* of *blazed* was pronounced as a final voiced consonant [d] rather than as a separate syllable as the spelling would indicate.

Of course, all the reasons given for Jeff's reading errors are edu-cated guesses rather than statements of unquestionable fact. The more a teacher sees the same types of errors repeated by a learning reader, the more confident she can be that they provide an accurate picture of the range of reading strategies employed by that learner. The analysis of one brief reading passage is not enough for con-fident generalizations. Jeff's reading in this passage does, however, suggest that he is capable of employing a wide range of reading strategies and that he is well on the way to proficient reading.

---

[10] This rule states in part that when a vowel grapheme is followed in the spelling by a single consonant and then another vowel, the first vowel grapheme is pronounced as a "long" vowel.

Private and Public Reading

For the beginner, reading is an oral procedure. Most new readers generally read out loud; oral reading seems to facilitate their efforts at deciphering a written text, since sounding out words is easier when the reader is making real sounds. Reading without making sounds is a more advanced skill requiring additional rather than less effort. So natural is the tendency to pronounce what one is reading that even silent readers move their vocal muscles as they read—that is, they subvocalize.

Vocalization of this sort is not a product of reading but rather a part of the process. When one reads privately, for one's own benefit, the ultimate product is comprehension. The following diagram represents the processes involved in "private" reading:

Private Reading

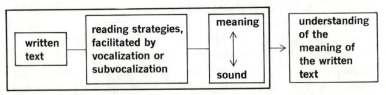

The sound-meaning association, which is the reader's language code or language competence, must be associated with and used to decipher the written text. Reading strategies such as the ones discussed earlier in this chapter provide a means for making this association. In private reading the duration of the decoding process is flexible; a reader is free to slow down on difficult passages which require more extensive applications of the various reading strategies. The vocalization produced in private reading reflects the process it is facilitating: incorrect as well as correct guesses are vocalized; misreadings and misunderstandings are spoken—and sometimes corrected orally as well. The vocalization of private reading is not and is not intended to be fluent grammatical English.

Fluent, grammatical oral reading is only possible when the reader already understands the meaning of what he is saying. Such fluent vocalization cannot be a part of the reading process; it is a secondary product of that process. This sort of reading for oral fluency can be called "public" reading:

Public Reading

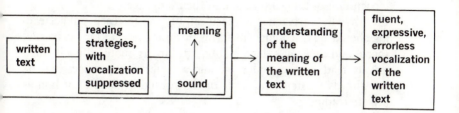

Public reading is more complicated than private reading in several ways. The public reader is under constant pressure to decode fast enough so that his vocalization will sound as rapid and fluent as speech. The decoding process itself is more complicated in public reading because experimental vocalization must be suppressed. Whereas private reading is primarily a passive skill, public reading requires an active command of the language, dialect, and style of the written text.

Children and most adults reading aloud with listeners present produce attempts at public reading that are interrupted by and blended with the vocalizations of private reading. The reading sample described in the preceding section of this chapter illustrates such a blending. In line 10, for example, Jeff vocalized his private struggle with the phrase *sweetened with wild honey*. Finally, when he came to understand the meaning of that phrase in its context, he went back and gave the phrase a fluent public reading.

A reading teacher cannot be effective unless he distinguishes between private and public reading. When the teacher of private reading listens to students read aloud, he tries to determine what reading strategies are being employed and how effectively and efficiently each is being used. He interrupts the reading process only to encourage the use of different strategies or to confirm some guess that the reader has made. His goal is to assist his students in becoming independent and successful in their application of reading strategies; he has succeeded when they understand what they are reading. Such a teacher is pleased when he hears students converting a sentence in the text into their own dialect, since such a conversion is possible only if they understand the meaning of the text. Similarly, the private-reading teacher is pleased when students pronounce a word according to their own pronunciation norms, even if such norms do not conform to those of the teacher or the author, since again the readers will have demonstrated a recognition of the word as one in their language.

Only when a teacher is specifically trying to teach public reading should he discourage all forms of misreading and insist on oral speed and fluency. Since public reading is more difficult than private reading, the student should attempt only passages that he has already mastered privately or that would be simple for him as private reading.

Educators generally place too much emphasis on public reading. Public reading is a special skill important to politicians, actors, and certain other adult occupational groups. But it is not equivalent to, nor should it be confused with, knowing how to read. Most adults —indeed, many teachers—are poor public readers.

Appendix

KEY TO PRONUNCIATION

Symbol	Key Words (corresponding graphemes italicized)	Dictionary Symbol
Consonants		
[b]	*b*oy, ca*b*	b
[č]	*ch*urch, *ch*ip, hat*ch*	ch
[d]	*d*ead, *d*o	d
[f]	*f*un, *f*air, o*ff*	f
[g]	*g*o, *g*ay, e*gg*	g
[h]	*h*ome, *h*ead	h
[ǰ]	*j*u*dg*e, *g*em, a*g*e	j
[k]	*k*ill, *k*i*ck*, *c*ome, *c*at	k
[l]	*l*et, *l*itt*l*e	l
[m]	*m*an, ha*m*	m
[n]	*n*o, ha*n*d	n
[ŋ]	si*ng*, si*ng*le, thi*n*k	ŋ
[p]	*p*ull, tri*p*	p
[r]	*r*ed, fa*r*	r

(Continued)

Source: Adapted from Bruce Cronnell, "Annotated Spelling-to-Sound Correspondence Rules," Southwest Regional Laboratory research memorandum, Inglewood, Calif., Sept. 26, 1969. Dictionary symbols are those used in *Webster's New World Dictionary* (1957). Reprinted by permission.

Symbol	Key Words (corresponding graphemes italicized)	Dictionary Symbol
[s]	*s*ee, i*c*e, mi*ss*	s
[š]	*sh*e, *s*ure, i*ss*ue, na*ti*on, has*h*	sh
[t]	*t*en, hi*t*, lik*ed*	t
[v]	*v*ase, lo*v*e	v
[w]	*w*et, lang*u*age, q*u*ick	w
[y]	*y*et, *y*ou	y
[z]	*z*oo, la*z*y, plea*s*e, wive*s*	z
[ž]	vi*s*ion, trea*s*ure	zh
[θ]	*th*ing, ba*th*	th
[ð]	*th*em, ba*th*e	<u>th</u>

Vowels

[i]	sc*e*ne, n*ea*t, s*ee*, chi*e*f	ē
[ɪ]	b*i*t, h*i*dden	i
[e]	n*a*me, d*ay*, th*ey*	ā
[ɛ]	g*e*t, h*ea*d	e
[æ]	f*a*t, b*a*d	a
[a]	h*o*t, c*a*r	o
[ɔ]	s*o*ng, l*o*ss, t*au*ght, l*a*wn, t*a*lk, b*a*ll, th*ou*ght	ô
[o]	b*o*ne, g*o*, f*o*rk, t*oe*, b*oa*rd, kn*ow*	ō
[ʊ]	p*u*t, p*u*sh, b*oo*k, c*ou*ld	oo
[u]	f*oo*d, d*ew*, t*u*ne	o͞o
[ə]	b*u*t, *a*bove (unstressed)	ə
	(stressed)	u
[ay]	cr*y*, m*i*ne, d*ie*	ī
[aw]	f*ou*nd, *ow*l	ou
[oy]	b*oy*, n*oi*se	oi

THE LINGUISTICS OF WRITING

During the years they spend in elementary and secondary school, children are still developing the ability to speak and understand their native language. They should be encouraged in their development of natural language skills and urged to acquire the ability to express such skills in writing; but the teacher who confuses these two types of learning and forces students to write in language they have not yet mastered is imposing a double burden. Since writing, like reading, involves an unnatural representation of natural language, teachers should never insist that students write in language they cannot use competently in speaking. Although this suggestion parallels the one made in Chapter 3 that students should not be forced to read language they cannot understand, the parallelism between teaching reading and teaching writing is not a complete one. Not only do such passive skills as understanding and reading develop ahead of their active counterparts, speaking and writing, but some passive skills—the ability to understand a wide range of different dialects, for example—are seldom if ever matched by their active counterparts. Of those individuals who understand several dialects of a language, few can speak fluently in more than one.

A teacher of composition should determine whether his students have the natural language skills necessary to produce the language he expects them to write. More specifically, he must judge whether they know the vocabulary and grammatical structures required by the subject matter; whether they command the register or style expected for that type of writing; and whether they have mastered the rules of strategy and appropriateness that indicate what style or stylistic variants should be employed in addressing the intended audience. Many writers, even at a fairly early age, try to use a more elevated style of language in their compositions than they normally use in conversation. Their first efforts in this direction are generally marked on the one hand by hypercorrect or stilted forms and on the other hand by lapses into less formal, more familiar styles. The student whose writing is erratic in this manner has recognized the need to use different styles of language in writing and is struggling to reproduce them. Teachers of composition should view these efforts as an important step toward the ability to write formal English—and therefore welcome rather than discourage them. Students made to feel ashamed or self-conscious about their early attempts at writing formal language may become reluctant to produce further evidence of their rudimentary command of this skill, and thus they may be seriously hindered in learning to perfect it.

Teachers who insist that their students use a foreign dialect in composition are imposing a severe, perhaps even an impossible, additional learning burden. Moreover, no dialect is inappropriate for composition or writing. What teachers generally consider inappropriate is not a dialect but an informal style of that dialect. Consequently, instead of trying to change their students' dialect, teachers could act more in accord with natural language learning tendencies by encouraging students to develop more formal writing styles in the dialect they are already using.

An Elementary-School Child's Perception of Formal, Literary English

A comparison of two versions of the same story told by Kathy, an eight-year-old third-grader, illustrates a child's emerging awareness of stylistic differences in English and supports the contention that some characteristics of formal, literary English can be mastered by preliterate or semiliterate elementary-school children. Kathy was asked to tell a familiar story, in her own words and at normal conversational speed. She chose "Cinderella," and her rendition of it was recorded on tape. This oral version of the story was supposed to be "practice" for a second, written version which would be typed exactly as Kathy dictated it. Although Kathy had related numerous stories out loud, she had never before been asked to produce this kind of extended "composed" story; she was scarcely able to read, let alone to write, either of the versions she narrated. Her knowledge of "Cinderella" came from at least four sources: the Walt Disney animated cartoon version of the story, a television production of the Rogers and Hammerstein musical adaptation, and two or more short storybook versions that had been read to her. Kathy's first version was told in the style of English she normally used when talking to her parents or other adults. In the dictated version, on the other hand, Kathy was consciously trying to elevate her style. She "composed" with deliberation, several times making stylistic "improvements" in sentences that she had previously dictated.

In the transcriptions of the Cinderella story that follow, obvious false starts and pauses have been omitted. Punctuation was, of course, supplied; but in all other respects these printed versions are as true as possible to the spoken originals.

KATHY'S "CINDERELLA"

Version 1
(told at conversational tempo)

Version 2
(dictated)

Once there was a girl that was named Cinderella. And she lived in a house with her stepsisters and her stepmother. And her stepmother was real bad to her. And she made her do all the work. And her stepsisters were mean and selfish at her. And then she was in the house, and her stepmother said, "Now you finish the house and we're going to go someplace." And they went someplace, and the prince came along. And then Cinderella said, "Would you like some water?" And then he said, "Oh, yes." And then she got some water. And then the step-

Once upon a time there lived a little girl named Cinderella. And there was the stepmother and the two stepsisters. They were very mean. The stepmother made Cinderella work all the time. And she could hardly rest. Then one day the stepmother said, "I am going to the store, and I want you to take care of the house." And while she was gone, a prince was riding. It was a hot day and the prince was getting thirsty. The prince asked Cinderella if he could have a drink of water. Cinderella answered at once. Then the stepmother came home. The

mother came back, and the messenger came, and he gave a message that the prince was having a ball, and then Cinderella couldn't go because her stepmother wouldn't let her; she had too much work to do. And so the mice fixed up all the clothes for her. And then the girl said, "No, that's mine; no, that's mine." And Cinderella was crying. Then she went in the garden and cried and then a fairy godmother came and said, "Don't fear because I'm going to help you make the things that you need. First of all, we need a pumpkin." And then she got a pumpkin. And then some mice and some . . . cats. And then the pumpkin became into horses, I mean the carriage, and the mice became into horses, and the cats became into men. And then they rode off, and then she said, "Wait! What about my clothes?" And then the fairy godmother goes bippity-boppity-boo, and she has lots of good clothes, and then her fairy godmother says, "You'd better be back by twelve because then the things will be all back to the pumpkin and the mice and the cats. And so she went to the ball and the prince said, "Oh, I love her." And then she danced with the prince, and then the clock struck twelve, and she ran, and she ran, and she ran home. And she dropped a slipper and the messenger said—and the king said, "Take this slipper until you find the person that matches the foot on the slipper." And then the messenger went, and then he dropped by house by house until finally he came to Cinderella's house. And then the stepmother stepmother said, "Did you let anyone in the house?" Cinderella answered, "No, but I did give a kind man a drink of water." The stepmother said, "You fool! I told you not to do that! Get back to work at once." One day a messenger came along. He was giving out invitations to the ball. Then the stepsister said, "Can we go, stepmother?" Then the stepmother said, "Of course you may go." And then Cinderella asked if she could go. The stepmother said, "No, you have too much work to do." Then the night of the ball came. The stepsisters were getting dressed for the ball. Cinderella was helping them zip and button. Then when it was time to go, Cinderella asked, "May I go?" The stepmother said, "You may not go. You have too much work to do." Then Cinderella went into the garden and wept. Then a shiny light came down, and it was a fairy godmother. Cinderella was scared at first, but then the fairy godmother said, "Don't be afraid, Cinderella. I am your fairy godmother." "Would you like to go to the ball?" said the fairy godmother. "Oh, yes, oh, yes," said Cinderella, "but I don't have anything." "Well, we'll take care of that," said the fairy godmother. "First we need a pumpkin." So Cinderella brought a pumpkin. "And next we need some mice." And Cinderella got the mice, too. "And then," said the fairy godmother, "we need some rats." And then Cinderella did just what she said. And at once the pumpkin became a carriage, and the mice became horses, and rats be-locked her up in her room. And then he tried it on one stepsister's foot, and it didn't go. And then she [sic] tried on the other stepsister's foot, but it didn't go. And then the mice by that time were —they sneaked the key out from the stepmother's pocket, and they brought, and they slipped it under the door. And then she got it and she said, "Wait! wait! How about me?" And then she tried it on, and it matched. And then when she put it on, she turned into all her beautiful clothes again. And they lived happily ever after.

came men. And then the fairy godmother said, "There's one thing we have forgotten." "What?" said Cinderella. "How about your clothes?" "Oh," said Cinderella. "We need a nice gown," said the fairy godmother. "And some nice glass slippers." "Oh, thank you," said Cinderella. Cinderella got in the carriage and was ready to go, but the fairy godmother stopped her, and said, "Wait, you have to be back by twelve o'clock." Then Cinderella got in her carriage and went. When the prince saw her, he was delighted, and danced with her all evening. Then the clock struck twelve, and Cinderella said, "I must be leaving now." And the prince said, "No! no! Cinderella. I want to dance with you some more. You're so pretty." And then Cinderella hurried out the door. And she dropped a slipper. And then she changed back into her old clothes again. And she hurried back home before her stepmother and stepsisters got home and started back to her work. Then the stepmother and stepsisters came home. The stepmother said, "Why aren't you finished with your work?" Cinderella said, "I guess I was just slow today." Then the stepmother and the stepsisters went up and got undressed. By that time at the palace, the prince had found the golden slipper that Cinderella had dropped. And the king said, "We must find that beautiful princess." And so the messenger brought the slipper around to the whole town. And then he came to Cinderella's house. The stepmother saw him, and she locked Cinderella up in a little room. The messenger tried the slipper on one of the step-sisters, and it wouldn't go on. He tried it on another stepsister, but it didn't go on either. By that time, the mice had taken the key from the stepmother's pocket and had slipped it under the door. Cinderella said, "Thank you, thank you," to the mice, and she ran down the stairs and said, "Wait! the slipper might fit my foot." Then the messenger slipped it on her foot, and it went on just right. Then, at that second, she turned into her beautiful gown again, and the prince and princess lived happily ever after. The end.

That these two renditions of "Cinderella" vary as they do sug-gests Kathy's awareness of the stylistic differences between conver-sational English and more formal, literary English. Determining the nature and extent of that awareness requires an analysis of specific changes Kathy was able to make in her use of language.

1. Perhaps the most striking difference between the two versions is in the use of coordinating conjunctions and of phrases that func-tion as coordinating conjunctions. In the first version, virtually every sentence but the first and those in direct quotations begins with one of five conjoining words or phrases: *and, then, and then, but,* and *and so.* In version 2, coordinating conjunctions and intro-ductory adverbial constructions are used more sparingly and—even given the smaller number of sentences that employ such construc-tion—the variety of conjoining words or phrases is far greater. The following thirteen occur: *and, then, and while, and then, but then, so, and next, and at once, but, when, and so, by that time, and then at that second.*

2. A number of stylistic word-order inversions associated with formal or literary prose occur in the second but not the first of these two versions of "Cinderella." For example, version 1 begins: "Once there was a girl that was named Cinderella"; whereas ver-sion 2 reads: "Once upon a time there lived a little girl named Cinderella." The inverted phrasing of the latter sentence—the

underlying subject placed after an intransitive verb preceded by the dummy subject *there*—is so common in children's stories that it amounts to a literary cliché. Such an inversion, however, would never occur in the conversational English of a third-grade child. Further examples of an inversion of the normal word order of spoken English occur in the placement of the phrase identifying the speaker of a direct quotation. The normal word order in spoken English, and the order that occurs throughout version 1, is: *X said,* ". . . ." Examples of this construction in version 1 include: *And then she said, "Wait! What about my clothes?"* or *And the king said, "Take this slipper. . . ."* Two ways of inverting this order occur at various points in Kathy's second version of "Cinderella": the speaker identified in the middle of the quotation: *"And then," said the fairy godmother, "we need some rats.";* and the speaker identified at the end of the quotation: *"Oh, thank you," said Cinderella.* In these two stylistic inversions Kathy quite properly reversed the order of the subject and verb: *Cinderella said,* becomes *said Cinderella.*

3. A subordinate clause functioning as an adverb of time occurs only once in the first version of the story: *And then when she put it on, she turned into all her beautiful clothes again.* The second version of the story contains a number of such constructions: *And while she was gone, a prince was riding . . . Then when it was time to go, Cinderella asked, "May I go?" . . . When the prince saw her, he was delighted, and danced with her all evening.* Instead of such preceding adverbial clauses, version 1 tends to use conjoined sentences· *And then she was in the house, and her step-mother said, "Now you finish the house and we're going to go someplace."*

4. In version 1, when two conjoined sentences share the same subject, that subject is almost always restated as a pronoun in the second of the two sentences. So, for example: *The messenger came, and he gave a message . . . And she ran, and she ran, and she ran home.* Version 2 omits such restatements of the subject more frequently and in more complex sentences: *When the prince saw her, he was delighted, and danced with her all evening . . . And she hurried back home before her stepmother and stepsisters got home and started back to her work . . . By that time, the mice had taken the key from the stepmother's pocket and had slipped it under the door.*

5. Beginning with *And then the fairy godmother goes bippity-boppity-boo* . . . , version 1 lapses for two or three sentences from its past tense into the present tense. No similar inconsistency occurs in version 2; there the past tense is used throughout the narrative.

6. In version 2 the verb *wept* is used in place of the first version's less literary verb *cried*. The second "Cinderella" also rejects the nonstandard construction *became into* (*the mice became into horses*) and replaces it with a more standard form (*the mice became horses*).

These stylistic differences between Kathy's renditions of "Cinderella" support two fundamental assumptions regarding the nature of formal or literary dialect learning by school-age children:

First, an almost entirely passive exposure to formal, literary English can lead to the ability to produce this style in "composed" prose. In her preschool and early school years, Kathy had heard hundreds of stories couched in the literary language of children's books. Her telling of "Cinderella" was, however, the first time that Kathy had occasion to produce an extended sample of this style of prose. Her performance clearly indicates that her passive assimilation of literary prose enabled her to produce an approximation of such prose herself, with little difficulty and no special training or encouragement.

Second, the ability to "compose" written English, as Kathy did in her second "Cinderella," is clearly separable from the mastery of such mechanics of written language as spelling and punctuation. Certainly, Kathy would have been totally unable to write down the accounts of "Cinderella" she told and scarcely able to read them.

Reading and Writing: Symbol-Sound Correspondences

Both reading and writing require the ability to associate the sounds of language with written symbols or letters representing those sounds. However, the direction of the association required in reading is the opposite of that required in writing: the reader begins with the written symbols of a language and must associate them with sounds in that language; the writer, on the other hand, begins with words as sounds and must represent them as sequences of written symbols. The previous chapter discussed four ways in which the association between symbols and sounds in English is more complex than a simple one-to-one correspondence. Of those four, a correspondence in which one symbol stands for several different sounds was shown to be the most difficult for readers, since it forces them to employ additional strategies for determining which of the possible sounds is the appropriate one for the word in question. For the writer-speller, on the other hand, this correspondence of one symbol to several sounds is not a major difficulty: since he begins with sounds, he can unhesitatingly assign a letter (albeit the same letter) to each of the different sounds involved in such a correspondence. The most complicated sound-symbol correspondence from his point of view is, rather, one in which a single sound can be represented by several different symbols or combinations of symbols. When this type of correspondence occurs, pronouncing the word does not lead the writer automatically and unambiguously to the correct spelling; therefore, he must devise and use other strategies for determining which of the conceivable spellings is the correct one.

Unfortunately for spellers of English, this one-symbol-to-many-sounds correspondence is extremely common in the language. The spelling of English vowel sounds is particularly notorious in this respect. In the chart on the following pages, the first column lists each of the vowel sounds found in English and the second gives the more common spellings used to represent that sound. Each spelling is then illustrated by an appropriate English word. The last column gives the relative frequency of each spelling in English. For example, 69.49, the first number in the column, indicates that for 69.49 percent of occurrences of the sound [a] in English words that sound is spelled o.

Even though their rare spellings are not listed, the chart shows that most English vowel sounds have at least two or three variant spellings. Faced with this range of choices, the speller might well seek out rules to help him determine which alternative spelling is appropriate for a given word. The preceding chapter's rules for deciding between alternative pronunciations in sounding out words are not the solution, however: the rules that work for readers do not work for spellers. The rules for readers describe the association between a single spelling and several different sounds whereas the

COMMON SPELLINGS FOR ENGLISH VOWEL SOUNDS

Sound	Spelling	Example	Frequency*
[a]	o	dot	69.49
	a	far	26.67
[æ]	a	cab	96.58
[e]	a	angel	44.57
	a–e	blade	35.14
	ai	aid	9.25
[ɛ]	e	bet	90.94
[i]	e	be	69.54
	ee	feel	9.81
	ea	eat	9.65
[i] or [ɪ]	e	hero	32.32
before r†	ea	hear	24.74
	ee	deer	18.18
	e–e	here	13.63
[ɪ]	i	did	68.40
	y‡	myth	23.04
[o]	o	both	72.51
	o–e	code	14.30
[ɔ]	o	cord	40.67
	a	wall	21.51
	au	faucet	19.03

Source: Compiled from material presented in Paul R. Hanna, Jean S. Hanna, Richard E. Hodges, and Edwin H. Rudorf, Jr., *Phoneme-Grapheme Correspondences as Cues to Spelling Improvement* (Washington, D.C.: U.S. Department of Health, Education, and Welfare, Office of Education, 1966).

* Spelling variants are listed in decreasing order of frequency. Frequency is represented as a percentage of the total occurrences of the sound in English words. Only those spelling variants necessary to account for 80 percent of the occurrences of each sound are included in this table.

† The exact pronunciation differs from one dialect of English to another.

‡ These figures are based on the assumption that the final *y* in words like *baby* and *happy* is pronounced [I].

Sound	Spelling	Example	Frequency*
[u]	oo	boot	38.18
	u	truth	20.52
	o	who	8.16
	u–e	rude	7.50
	ou	soup	6.40
[ʊ]	u	put	54.34
	oo	book	30.97
[ʌ] or [ɔ]§	u	cut	85.95
[ə]‖	o	carton	26.79
	a	canal	23.91
	i	pencil	22.40
	e	angel	12.68
[ɚ]#	e	her	39.77
	u	burn	25.79
	i	bird	13.21
	o	word	6.73
[ɚ]	e	after	76.77
	o	honor	12.35
[aw]	ou	out	55.91
	ow	howl	29.31
[ay]	i–e	like	37.44
	i	find	37.38
	y	by	14.23
[oy]	oi	coil	61.74
	oy	boy	32.31
[yu]	u	union	68.51
	u–e	use	21.54

§ The exact pronunciation differs from one dialect of English to another. These figures represent occurrence in stressed syllables only.

‖ These figures represent occurrence in unstressed syllables only.

Retroflex [r] occurs as the vocalic nucleus of syllables in American English. Occurrences of this sound in stressed and unstressed syllables are tabulated separately.

rules for spellers must describe the associations between a single sound and several different spellings. Moreover, the rules for reading a given word base the pronunciation of one letter upon the presence or absence in that word of various other *letters*, while those for spelling must specify how each sound in a word should be spelled based on the presence or absence of other *sounds*.

A reader can, for example, predict the pronunciation of the letter *c* in a given word by referring to the letter that follows it in that word. Among the rules he would have to know is one that says: the letter *c* is pronounced [s] when it is followed either by the letter *e* or by the letter *i*. This rule does not relate the sound of the letter *c* to other *sounds* in the word; nor should it, since the reader will not be certain of those sounds until after he has succeeded in sounding out the word. He cannot assume that the letter *e*, for instance, will always represent the same sound—or any sound at all for that matter. Consider the words *ceiling, center,* and *nice*; the rule for the pronunciation of the letter *c* when it precedes the letter *e* applies in all three words even though the phonetic value of the letter *e* differs in each one.

A speller, however, is not concerned with pronouncing letters but with symbolizing sounds. For example, he may know that the sound [s] is usually spelled *s, c,* or *ss*. He may know, in addition, that it can be spelled *c* only if that *c* is followed by the letter *e* or the letter *i*. But how useful is this knowledge? How is he to be sure of the other letters in a word before he spells it? Even if he is certain that the letter following the one representing the sound [s] is an *e* or an *i*, he does not necessarily know that the sound [s] is spelled *c*; he only knows it *may* be spelled *c*. What the speller obviously needs is a rule by which he can determine precisely which letter represents the sound [s] in the word he is trying to spell, given only the knowledge of which he is certain—that is, his knowledge of the other sounds in his pronunciation of that word. In a language spelled on the basis of such rules, all choices between letters representing the same sound could be made by noting the position of that sound relative to other sounds in the word. Unfortunately, this state of affairs seldom exists in English.

Consider the following widely taught and widely known "rule" of English spelling: i *before* e *except after* c *or when sounded as* [e] *as in* neighbor *and* weigh. In order to apply this rule the speller must already know a great deal about the spelling of the word he is trying to spell. First, he must know that it involves the sound [i] spelled either *ie* or *ei*, even though neither spelling is the most common representation of that sound. In only 2.2 percent of its occurrences in English words is the sound [i] spelled *ie*, and it is represented by the sequence *ei* in less than 1 percent of its occurrences. To make matters worse, the rule has several exceptions (for example, *neither* and *seize*), and if the speller attempts to apply it to sounds other than [i]—and nothing in the rule itself prevents him from doing so—exceptions abound (*forfeit, stein, their,* and so on). Indeed, the rule seems to make only two exceptionless generalizations about English spelling: the sound [e] is never spelled *ie* and the phonetic sequence [si] is never spelled *cie*. And a study of every English word may show that even these generalizations have exceptions; moreover, at their best, they are only minimally helpful negative rules since each excludes a particular spelling but does not predict the proper one.

But even if the "*i* before *e*" rule were exceptionless and applicable to a large number of English words, the English speller would still have difficulty applying it. The rule requires that he know whether or not the sound before [i] in the word in question is spelled *c*. However, the speller begins with sounds, not letters, and is likely to have ignored the spelling *c* in favor of *s*, a more common representation of the sound [s]; given a confusion of these two spellings the "*i* before *e*" rule becomes nearly useless. This sort of ineffectuality would be eliminated if the rule followed the principle stated above: rules of spelling should relate the spelling of a sound to neighboring sounds rather than to neighboring letters. Restating the "*i* before *e*" rule in terms of neighboring sounds (*i* before *e* except after [s] . . .) makes it more widely applicable—additional words, such as *seize*, are accounted for—but new exceptions, such as *siege*, are created.

The last half of the rule—*or when sounded as* [e] *as in* neighbor *and* weigh—is, from the speller's point of view, a rule in itself, one that concerns the spelling of the sound [e] rather than the sound [i]. Unfortunately, this second rule has drawbacks similar to those of the first one: the spellings *ei* and *ie* are only two of fourteen possible English spellings for the sound [e], and this rule gives the speller no help at all in eliminating the other twelve possibilities.

In its original version the "*i* before *e*" rule seems useful only to those spellers who have all but mastered the words to which the rule does apply. If the speller is sure that the [i] vowel sound in question is represented by the letters *ei* or *ie* rather than by any of the more likely possibilities, and if he has spelled correctly the preceding consonant sound or at least properly eliminated the letter *c* as a possibility, then the rule may be of some help to him. But under no circumstances does it help in answering the more basic question: are the letter combinations *ei* and *ie* involved in the correct spelling at all?

Good spellers and good spelling teachers have long recognized another useful aid to spellers. Although English spelling frequently uses different and unpredictable letters to represent a given sound, it generally uses only one spelling for any given morpheme, regardless of how that morpheme is pronounced and whether it constitutes an entire word or only part of a word. If a writer knows how to spell a morpheme as it appears in one English word, he can predict, with considerable accuracy, how that same morpheme will be spelled in its other appearances in the language. The English past tense morpheme, for example, is consistently spelled *-ed* regardless of whether it is pronounced [t] as in *hoped*, [d] as in *seemed*, or [əd] as in *wanted*; the spelling *photo* occurs in both *photography* and *photographic*; and, with the exception of a predictable change in the final vowel, the spelling of *define* is retained in *definition*.

An awareness of this tendency toward morpheme consistency is particularly useful when a speller is trying to determine which vowel letter a given word uses in representing the unstressed vowel sound: schwa [ə]. Such an unstressed vowel occurs in the first syllable of *photography* ([fətagrəfi]), in the second syllable of *photographic* ([fotəgræfɪk]), and in the second syllable of *definition* ([dɛfənɪšən]). The puzzled speller of any of these syllables could determine the appropriate vowel for the schwa sound by remembering a word in which that same syllable is pronounced with full stress. For the schwa sounds in *photography* and *photographic* he might think of the word *photo*; for the one in *definition*, the word *define*.

Using morpheme identification to determine spelling is helpful but not flawless. It prompts many writers to confuse the spellings *-cede* and *-ceed* in the words *proceed* and *precede*, for example, and is probably often responsible for such misspellings as *repeati-*

tion. Also, this technique for predicting the spelling of a morpheme can be used only if the speller has encountered and recognized that same morpheme in a word he can spell. A student may, for example, use, spell, and understand the word *composition* without realizing that it shares a morpheme with *compose.*

Reading and Writing: Feedback Strategies

For a reader of English, feedback strategies provide perhaps the most useful single aid in decoding written texts. As was suggested in Chapter 3, the reader knows that his sounding out has been successful when: first, the sounds he has made form a word in his language; second, that word is grammatically appropriate for the context; and finally, that word is meaningful in that context. None of these three forms of feedback is available to the speller of English; natural language abilities are no help in confirming a possible spelling for English words. This fact, perhaps more than any other, makes writing English more difficult than reading it.

The kinds of feedback available to the speller are much weaker and vary greatly in effectiveness from one speller to another. Spellers with good visual memories can visualize the written form of a word and compare the way they are spelling it with their recollection of the correct spelling. Those who rely on this form of feedback generally cannot decide whether a word is spelled correctly until they see it written down. If you ask them how to spell some word, they will first write it out and then announce the spelling.

But some people are not good at visualizing the spelling of words, and for them this form of feedback is ineffective. They must depend on other clues, such as sound—not the sound of the word itself but the sound of the sequence of letters when the word is spelled aloud. Readers who use this form of feedback are generally very good at identifying words when they hear the spelling; in writing, they frequently repeat the letters of words to themselves.

Other forms of spelling feedback tend to be more complicated and usually require special skills or knowledge. The speller of English who can read and write French, Latin, or Spanish usually finds that his knowledge of this second language is helpful in spelling English words: many English words have been borrowed from these languages and often retain all or part of their original foreign spelling. A familiarity with several dialects of English can also be used to confirm spelling guesses since a correct spelling may be sounded more faithfully in one dialect than in another. For example, the spelling *gh* in words like *night* and *right* represents an actual sound in the English spoken in Scotland but not in other dialects of the language.

In view of the many difficulties inherent in English spellings, teachers should not become impatient with bad spellers. The American habit of scoffing at poor spellers is not in the best interests of education. More positively, since different spellers seem to base their spelling on different forms of feedback, teachers of spelling should help each individual student find the form of feedback, either visual or aural, that works best for him.

Grammar and Punctuation

The rules for punctuation in English typically employ formal grammatical terms. Thus, for example, there are rules specifying that: when a *dependent* or *subordinate clause* precedes an *independent* or *main clause*, the two clauses are separated by commas; a *nonrestrictive relative clause* is set off by commas whereas a *restrictive relative clause* is not; when two *independent clauses* are joined by a *coordinating conjunction*, a comma precedes that conjunction. To follow such rules, the writer must be able to recognize dependent and independent clauses, relative clauses (both restrictive and nonrestrictive), and coordinating conjunctions. All students, even first-graders, have mastered the grammatical concepts described by these terms. Knowing *how* to interpret and produce these grammatical forms does not, however, imply knowing *about* them—that is, for instance, knowing what they should be called. During a child's first years in school his knowledge of grammar is and must be automatic and unconscious. Only later, in learning how to punctuate sentences in writing, must he begin to make conscious certain aspects of this unconscious linguistic knowledge.

The bringing to consciousness of unconscious grammatical knowledge is no easy task, for this knowledge tends to be extremely complex. For example, in order to differentiate dependent and independent clauses, the writer must understand consciously (that is, know *about*) the different functions of coordinating and subordinating conjunctions, various restrictions in the sorts of auxiliary verbs or verb phrases that can occur in different types of clauses, and a set of rules that distinguish sentences from clauses and clauses from phrases or words. Linguists marvel that children are able to master this complex set of grammatical interactions. But teachers tear their hair in frustration when attempting to make such complex interactions part of the conscious knowledge of elementary-school and secondary-school students. Successful teachers soon learn that the best teaching procedure may be to encourage students to develop intuitive shortcuts for clause recognition and differentiation: *If it can stand alone, it is a main clause. If it needs another clause to complete the thought, then it is a subordinate clause.* Such rules-of-thumb work because students already have an intuitive grasp of which sequences of words in their language can stand alone and which cannot.

Some educators view the teaching of punctuation as a justification for teaching grammar. Debates rage over which grammar—traditional, structural, or transformational—is best for this classroom use. But such debates seem groundless since any of the current approaches to grammatical description can provide the odds and ends needed to master the rules of English punctuation. A comprehensive study of English grammatical structure, regardless of approach, is a waste of class time *if* the ultimate objective is to teach punctuation.

Because punctuation is associated with grammatical structure, teachers are unfortunately inclined to confuse a lack of knowledge about punctuation with an inability to produce grammatical English. The teacher exclaims, "That poor child doesn't even know how to write a complete English sentence," and decides to assign the student a massive dose of English grammar. In almost all such cases the child in reality knows how to and indeed does write grammatical English sentences but puts the punctuation marks in the wrong places or leaves them out entirely. A minor problem is treated as a major failing. In the following composition, the writer seems to lack all knowledge of punctuation except the rule that the whole thing begins with a capital letter and ends with a period. However, the entire composition is made up of grammatical English sentences; this can be proved by inserting the appropriate punctuation marks.

> My favourite television programme is Bewitched one day she went to see her new house and her mother just waved her hand and there was trees and flowers all over the garden then they went into the house and she wobeld her nose and it was all furnished but she had married a human and she promised that she would not use her witchcraft again and she would by all her furniture and plant all the plants by seeds.[1]

As long as the sentences a student writes can be punctuated properly by adding or subtracting punctuation marks, the problem is a minor one. Only when the student's writing cannot be punctuated so as to delimit complete sentences is he writing sentence fragments; and only when he himself cannot recognize and correct such sentence fragments is there any real cause for concern over his mastery of natural language-learning skills.

Some Suggestions for Composition Teachers

Linguists do not hold a magic key for teachers of composition. Many, indeed most, of the arsenal of skills that a fluent writer must command are outside the linguist's area of specialization. Therefore this chapter has not discussed the choosing of subject matter or the organizing of subject matter; principles governing these tasks have been codified by rhetoricians and logicians. No mention has been made here of the physical skills involved in writing: for example, the muscular control necessary to print, write, or even type letters. No mention has been made here of the physical format of the written page: matters of letter shape, spacing, margins, and indenting. Without making any claims to completeness, then, here are four suggestions to composition teachers that reflect the linguist's special vantage on language.

First, when the composition skills are natural language skills, encourage learning through the use of such natural language-learn-

---

[1] This essay, written by a twelve-year-old British boy, is recorded in Hugh Fraser, "The Teaching of Writing," in *Applied Linguistics and the Teaching of English*, ed. Hugh Fraser and W. R. O'Donnell (New York: Humanities Press, 1969), pp. 121–39.

ing techniques as were discussed in Chapter 2. Such techniques are particularly useful in teaching students to recognize which styles of English are appropriate for different sorts of subject matter and for different audiences. Natural language-learning techniques are also appropriate for helping students to master these various styles of English, first as passive, then as active, language skills.

Second, separate component composition skills and focus the learner's attention on each skill separately. Writing is, from a linguistic point of view, an extremely complex task involving virtuosity in language production displayed in conjunction with complex rules for punctuation and (in English) an inefficient spelling system. Add to these the tasks of getting words down on paper in a legible form and communicating something through this complex system, and it becomes evident how great an accomplishment writing is and how easy it is for learners of writing to become discouraged. In the early stages of learning how to write, mistakes are an inevitable and natural part of the learning experience. Students who are told that they must avoid all mistakes soon discover that no amount of effort will produce what the teacher expects. And so, all too frequently, they become totally discouraged and give up trying to communicate through writing. To avoid this tragedy, teachers must separate the task of learning to write into: learning to punctuate, learning to spell, learning to use different styles of English appropriately, learning to select and organize subject matter, learning to form letters, and learning to write in straight horizontal lines with straight vertical margins. The teacher who corrects, or forces students to correct, all types of composition errors on every theme may not be acting in his students' best interest. Using each theme to focus a student's attention on a single aspect of composition and rewarding mastery of that one aspect is much more instructive than returning every theme covered with a discouraging maze of red marks.

Third, separate the task of learning how to sound out words from the task of learning how to spell those same words. As the preceding discussion demonstrates, these are indeed different tasks. The teacher who assumes that his students should be able to spell any word they can read is grossly mistaken and naive about the complex differences between word recognition and spelling.

Finally, use each student's written work as a basis for recognizing his particular successes and failures in composition. Do not assume that all students learn to spell, punctuate, or use formal English in the same way or in the same sequence. Further, do not prescribe a course in English grammar as a panacea for bad writers. All current evidence suggests that learning about English grammar does little to make the student who writes badly write better. Only when a writer is at an advanced stage in the mastery of composition skills should he begin to consider consciously the precise grammatical structures of the sentences he uses and the varieties of grammatical options that are available to him in his compositions.[2] For less advanced writers, such complex considerations can only lead to confusion and discouragement.

---

[2] The value of English linguistics for advanced-composition students is discussed further in Chapter 8.

LANGUAGE ATTITUDES
LANGUAGE VARIATION
AND STANDARD ENGLISH

As a student continues to mature linguistically during his early school years, he becomes increasingly adept at distinguishing different ways of speaking his native language; the elementary-school student can generally spot accents foreign to his own and is often able to imitate them to some extent. In addition to sharpening his ear for accents, the school experience encourages a student to perceive (and ultimately to assume) the complex sets of attitudes his society holds toward different accents, styles, and dialects of its language. He learns to consider some ways of speaking "correct" or "proper" and to judge others "sloppy," "careless," or "substandard." Most of American society seems to approve of this sort of linguistic labeling and expects English teachers and textbooks to train students to distinguish "good" English from "bad" English so that they can opt for the former.

Linguists, who have a special vantage from which to view both language variation and attitudes toward it, have for some years questioned the rationality of these attitudes. Some linguists have gone beyond academic questioning to campaign actively for changes in the way dictionaries are written and grammar is presented to students. Opposing factions within American education have called for the maintenance of traditional standards in language and have accused linguists of supporting a sort of stylistic permissiveness that threatens the purity, beauty, or expressiveness of English. But, unable to find linguistic evidence for the claim that one way of speaking English is purer, more beautiful, or more expressive than another, linguists continue to question the rationality of dictionaries and grammars that maintain arbitrary standards of correctness. Consumers of such dictionaries and grammars, who are under social pressure to conform to traditional language standards however arbitrary they may be, have been disturbed by attempts to divest these references of their function as arbiters of linguistic correctness. To understand both positions in this debate, one must consider, on the one hand, the linguistic evidence concerning language variation and, on the other, the pressure for linguistic conformity within American society and the doctrine of linguistic correctness.[1]

Variations in Style

Knowing how to speak English involves knowing how to adjust one's speech to suit the audience and the occasion; it is a matter of knowing not simply how to use formal English but also *when* to use it. Anyone who fails to use formal English when it is appropriate is likely to be accused of acting undignified; the speaker who uses a formal style of language in an informal situation is probably "putting on airs" and should be considered no less reprehensible.

Most speakers of English have learned both formal and informal ways of expressing the same idea. Compare, for example: *With whom did you wish to speak?* and *Who do ya wanna talk to?* These two questions have the same basic meaning, but their differing connotations place them at opposite stylistic poles; the first question is formal to the point of coldness, the second informal

[1] For an excellent documentation of this debate in progress see James Sledd and Wilma R. Ebbitt, eds., *Dictionaries and That Dictionary* (Chicago: Scott, Foresman and Co. 1962), a collection of articles and essays on the controversy surrounding the publication of *Webster's Third New International Dictionary.*

to the point of rudeness. Part of this stylistic polarity has to do with vocabulary. The important difference between the words *with* and *to, wish* and *want,* and *speak* and *talk* is not that they mean different things but that they mean the same thing with different degrees of formality. But vocabulary is not the only linguistic indicator of a change in style: grammar and pronunciation also change with increasing or decreasing formality. Using the past tense *did* rather than the present *do,* or the object case *whom* rather than the subject case *who,* or placing the preposition at the beginning rather than at the end of the sentence—all signal connotational, stylistic differences rather than denotational differences in "dictionary meaning." The pronunciation change from "you" [yu] to "ya" [yə] or from "want to" [wanttu] to "wanna" [wanə] changes not the meaning of the words but their stylistic value.

Of course the speaker of English is not limited to a choice between two stylistic extremes. By choosing a combination of formal and informal variants, a speaker of English can convey more subtle degrees of formality. For example, the substance of the two questions discussed above might also be expressed as

> Who did you want to talk with?

or

> To whom do you want to speak?

Not all combinations of formal and informal variants are possible, however. For example, the sentence

> *With who did ya wanna speak?

is clearly ungrammatical (the initial asterisk is how linguists commonly denote this fact): not only would style manuals inveigh against it but speakers of English who never open a style manual would also consider it laughably unspeakable.

English-speaking adults have generally assimilated the grammatical rules governing stylistic variation, but young school children usually have not. As suggested in Chapter 2, stylistic variation is among those natural language skills that children are still in the process of acquiring during their school years. Since they lack exposure to the situations that teach formal language variants, children just beginning their schooling tend to be fluent in only the informal range of their language.

Dialect Variation

A different dimension of language variation cuts across the dimension of style change. Northerners and southerners, Bostonians and New Yorkers, Mexican Americans and Afro-Americans, regardless of what style they may be using, speak different dialects of English. The term *dialect* as it is used by linguists has no derogatory overtones. All varieties of a language are called dialects of that language, and consequently, anyone who speaks a language speaks a dialect of that language. Any group of people within the general English-speaking population who are in frequent verbal communication and identify themselves as members of the same social group may develop and perpetuate a distinctive dialect of English. In societies with limited geographic mobility, dialects are associated with different geographic regions. In societies with limited socioeconomic or interethnic mobility, social or ethnic dialects develop. In a society as large and complex as the United States, dialect differences may separate geographic, socioeconomic, or ethnic groups, and to some extent age groups and occupational groups as well.

Anyone listening to a strange dialect for the first time is most likely to be struck by differences in the way some words are pronounced and will probably refer to such differences as an accent. President Kennedy was noted for a New England accent because he pronounced *vigor* as "vigga" and *Cuba* as "cubar." But, for a linguist, noting differences in the pronunciation of individual words is only a first step; such isolated differences are only clues to more general distinctions in a dialect's rules of pronunciation. For example, the retroflex "r" sound common in American English is pronounced by New Englanders only when it occurs in the part of the syllable that precedes the vowel. Where most other speakers of American English use the retroflex "r" sound after vowels, New Englanders use a modified vowel sound; that is, they say "vigga" for *vigor*, "pahk" for *park*, and "cah" for *car*. Equally distinctive is their use of the retroflex "r" sound to ease the transition between a word that ends with a vowel and another that begins with a vowel. Thus, when spoken by a New Englander, the phrase *Cuba is* becomes "Cuba-r-is." This combination of rules, replacing a vowel sound followed by "r" with a modified vowel sound and adding "r" between two vowel sounds separated by a word boundary, delights other Americans, who perceive perverse New Englanders leaving out "r" where it belongs and putting it in where it doesn't. In the linguist's view, however, far from indicating verbal sloppiness or perversity, these practices demonstrate an adherence to a different set of phonological rules.

In addition to its unique phonological rules, any given dialect may also employ its own rules of grammar. Consider the phenomenon of multiple negation, for instance. In somewhat simplified terms, those dialects that employ multiple negation negate a sentence by including a negative marker wherever it is possible to do so. In most sentences there is only one such opportunity—at the verb; and the marker used is either *not* or *-n't*:

$$\text{Bill has seen the movie.} \xRightarrow[\text{neg.}]{\text{mult.}} \text{Bill hasn't seen the movie.}$$

$$\text{Bill will tell me the truth.} \xRightarrow[\text{neg.}]{\text{mult.}} \text{Bill will not tell me the truth.}$$

However, when a positive sentence contains one or more "some" words—*somebody, someone, something,* and *sometimes*—additional opportunities for negation exist. Each of these words has a negative form, and in multiple-negation dialects this form appears along with a negated verb:

$$\text{Somebody will tell me something.} \xRightarrow[\text{neg.}]{\text{mult.}} \text{Nobody won't tell me nothing.}[2]$$

$$\text{Bill will sometimes tell someone something.} \xRightarrow[\text{neg.}]{\text{mult.}} \text{Bill won't never tell nobody nothing.}$$

Thus, such sentences as

*Bill won't ever tell me anything.

and

*Nobody will ever tell me the truth.

---

[2] For many speakers of multiple-negating dialects of American English, this sentence would be converted by further grammatical rules to the form *Won't nobody tell me nothing.*

would be considered ungrammatical in dialects that employ only multiple negation.

Single-negation dialects include a negative marker only once in any given sentence, normally at the first appropriate point. If a "some" word occurs beyond this point in the sentence, that word's first syllable is generally changed to "any" when the sentence is negated:

$$\text{Somebody will tell me something.} \xrightarrow[\text{neg.}]{\text{sing.}} \text{Nobody will tell me anything.}$$

$$\text{Bill will sometimes tell someone something.} \xrightarrow[\text{neg.}]{\text{sing.}} \text{Bill won't ever tell anyone anything.}$$

After studying such phenomena as multiple negation and the New England retroflex "r" in a wide range of social and regional dialects, linguists have concluded that: although the rules that govern the syntax or pronunciation of one dialect may differ from the rules that govern the syntax or pronunciation of another, all dialects are equally regular—that is, they are spoken according to equally complex and binding sets of grammatical and phonological rules.

The contention that from a linguistic point of view dialects are equally complex and regular places linguists at odds with current popular opinion on dialect variation, especially when the consideration is the dialectal differences between social classes or castes. In the musical *My Fair Lady* Professor Henry Higgins echoes popular sentiment when he berates lower-class Londoners for "speaking English any way they like." "Nonsense! Professor Higgins," a more modern linguist might respond: "The speech of Eliza Doolittle and her comrades has its own grammatical rules, and they are just as binding upon her as your dialect's rules are upon you."

Most adult speakers of English have mastered the range of styles associated with the dialect they normally speak; but rarely does an individual control the full stylistic range of two dialects. To the extent that a speaker masters a second dialect, his ability to use his original dialect generally decreases; indeed, complete changes of dialect are fairly common. Most of the speakers who seem bidialectal—for example, the professional comedians who specialize in dialect humor—are actually capable of only a monostylistic imitation of a second dialect. Unlike its true speakers, a dialect's imitators are seldom able to execute the subtle linguistic shifts that are necessary if it is to be used in varied situations.

Most imitations of a New York City accent replace all the "th" sounds [θ] and [ð] with "t" [t] and "d" [d] respectively, whereby *these things* ends up sounding like "dese tings." This exclusive use of the sounds [t] and [d] is an exaggeration, however. For actual speakers of New York City English the possible pronunciations of "th" include the fricative sounds [ð] and [θ] as well as the stop sounds [d] and [t]. Moreover, the fricative sounds of "th" are considered more formal than the stop sounds [d] and [t], and therefore the relative frequency of these two types of "th" sounds depends upon the style (and, hence, upon the situation) in which a New Yorker happens to be speaking.

Perhaps part of the reason imitators of a dialect oversimplify its complex variations is that speakers of dialect A are conscious that someone is using dialect B only when the speaker of dialect B uses some variant that does not occur in dialect A. Otherwise the speakers of dialect A are conscious only of the meaning the speaker of B is trying to convey, not the language he is using to do so. A speaker of Chicago English, for example, has only the pronunciation [ð] in words where a speaker of New York English can choose between [ð] and [d]. A Chicagoan listening to a New Yorker will pay no attention to the pronunciation of the word *this* as long as the New Yorker uses the variant [ðɪs]; if the New Yorker says [dɪs], however, the Chicagoan will immediately notice the pronunciation, and perhaps conclude that New Yorkers *always* pronounce the word *this* as "dis."

This tendency to generalize the differences between dialects and to ignore ways in which they overlap can have an unfortunate influence upon teaching procedures. For example, the Chicago public schools, in an attempt to teach standard Chicago English to students who speak a local variant of black southern English, train them to distinguish between "everyday talk" and "school talk."[3] Thus, for example, *I ain't* is labeled everyday talk while *I'm not* is labeled school talk. But what the writers of the program's teaching materials fail to realize is that in conversations out of school most of these students hear both *I ain't* and *I'm not* and that

[3] Board of Education, City of Chicago, *Psycholinguistic Oral Language Program: A Bi-dialectal Approach*, experimental edition, part 1 (1968).

many, if not all, of them use both these negative forms when speaking their original dialect. The assumption that "everyday talk" can be defined as only those variants of the nonstandard dialect that are not part of the school dialect is invalid; moreover, it is a misrepresentation that is bound to confuse the students. Even the youngest ones will come to realize that what is called everyday talk does not include the complete range of language they hear and use outside of school. Such a misrepresentation may be equally confusing for the teacher; for it prompts him to see his job as a matter of replacing one form, *I ain't*, with a totally new one, *I'm not*. In reality, however, a teacher of standard English as a second dialect must encourage his students to inhibit their use of one of two variant forms occurring within their dialect.

Community Attitudes Toward Language Variation

Many Americans mistakenly assume that linguists are in the business of establishing and maintaining rules of correctness. In fact, the linguist's rules are meant to describe how people actually speak; when the speakers of a language begin to violate such rules, it is the rules rather than the speakers that need changing. The rules that govern what nonlinguists think of as "correct" English, on the other hand, constitute an external standard that has been imposed upon the language with little regard to the ways in which it is actually spoken. Based on admonitions that began in early childhood, most Americans have the notion that there is a single correct way to speak English and that deviations from this standard are signs of ignorance or carelessness, and, in either case, to be avoided in their own speech and frowned upon in the speech of others. Accordingly, as parents, they assume that one of the English teacher's primary responsibilities is to "correct" the speech of the children they place in his or her care; thus, the doctrine of correctness continues.

Sociolinguists interested in understanding the language attitudes shared by speakers of English have made this doctrine of correctness in language an object of particular study. They have learned that a speaker's concept of correct English does not necessarily vary with the dialect of English that he himself uses. For example,

a study of language and language attitudes in New York City produced evidence that although New Yorkers speak English in a
wide variety of ways, they agree on how one should speak it. Presented with two variant ways of saying the same thing, all the subjects chose the same variant as the "correct" one, even though
many acknowledged that it was not the variant they usually used.[4]

The earlier example—*With whom did you wish to speak?/Who
do ya wanna talk to?*—illustrated the fact that stylistic variation
often involves an alternation between a more formal and a less
formal variant of the same semantic unit, each of which is appropriate in different situations. However, when confronted with two
such variants, most speakers of English will consistently choose as
"correct" the more formal stylistic variant, without considering the
circumstances under which it is to be used. In informal situations,
therefore, the doctrine of correctness is apt to conflict with the
need for stylistic appropriateness. For example, during the 1950s
Arthur Godfrey acted as host for a television program called
"Talent Scouts"; guests, acting as talent scouts, chatted with him
on camera before presenting the amateur they had brought to perform. At some point in the interview with each talent scout
Godfrey would ask, "Who did you bring for us?" This question
persisted until one irate listener wrote to the station informing
Godfrey that he had been using incorrect grammar; the question
should be "Whom did you bring for us?" Godfrey apologized
publicly for this "mistake" and in all future broadcasts carefully
enunciated a final -*m* on the interrogative pronoun. In doing so,
Godfrey—and presumably the producers and viewers of the show
as well—accepted the claim of grammatical correctness over a
sense of stylistic appropriateness: since Godfrey's manner as a host
included a relaxed casual rapport with his viewers, his use of *who*
was stylistically far more appropriate than his studied use of the
formal variant *whom*.

Speakers of English also associate linguistic correctness with
dialect status. In the United States, linguistic variants occurring in
the dialects spoken by Americans at high socioeconomic levels
are generally viewed as more correct than variants occurring only
in the dialects of groups at the lower end of the socioeconomic

---

[4] William Labov, "Social Evaluation," in *The Social Stratification of English in New York City* (Washington, D.C.: Center for Applied Linguistics,
1966), pp. 403–503.

scale. For the most part, good or correct English is taken to mean upper-class English, and conversely, bad or sloppy English is taken to mean lower-class English.

One popular characterization of "good" or "standard" English is that it is the variety of English spoken by the educated. Since in this country the ability to speak standard English is a prerequisite for admission to and success in institutions of higher learning, this description of good English has become something of a self-fulfilling prophecy. Moreover, those who equate good English with education forget that many *un*educated people, because of their socioeconomic background, speak "good English" and that being educated is not the same as sounding educated.

Professor Higgins is certainly correct when he remarks, "The moment an Englishman speaks . . . he makes some other Englishman despise him." For American speakers of English this remark can be extended even further: not only does an American, by his variety of English, make other Americans despise him, but he may even belittle himself for the way he speaks. Many Americans are convinced that there is one correct way to speak English but are at the same time uneasily aware that it is not the way *they* speak. An individual caught in such a linguistic trap is likely to develop neurotic attitudes toward his way of speaking. Since they are supposed to be members of the inner circle who know what correct English really is, English teachers can expect to encounter these attitudes frequently, both in and out of school. When he mentions his occupation to a group of new acquaintances, for instance, the English teacher may hear such apologies as "Well, I never was very good at grammar" and "I guess I've forgotten just about all of the grammar I ever knew." Then the conversation dwindles to an embarrassed, self-conscious silence.

The English Teacher's Response to Language Attitudes

No single easy response is possible to the complex problems that can be created for teachers by the language attitudes within a community. But every teacher in formulating his response to language differences should keep a few facts in mind. First, teachers must be aware that they themselves, as members of the community they serve, share many of its attitudes toward language. English teachers are especially prone to strong attitudes on linguistic purity and correctness; many chose their profession because of a deep love and respect for the beauty of the English language and of its literature. Understandably, English teachers often come to percieve as most beautiful and desirable those standard forms of English in which this great literature has principally been written.

Since English teachers are expected to be guardians of language standards and correctness, it is only natural that they tend to play the role assigned to them. The teacher of English who catches himself committing some linguistic faux pas—even when he is off duty and speaking unofficially and privately—is likely to feel a sense of guilt. If he were to reject publicly the role of language guardian, he might feel more at ease with himself but would probably arouse the same sort of concern among school administrators, parents, and some students that a drunken minister causes among church elders and members of his congregation.

Some teachers echo another popular notion of language by equating standard English use with intellectual potential and achievement when evaluating their students. The teacher who accuses students of using "sloppy diction" or of speaking "carelessly" and comments on the "unsatisfactory language experience in their home background," must be particularly careful that he or she is not simply denouncing them for their dialect differences. A child is not being sloppy when he speaks according to the linguistic rules of his own dialect; nor is he deprived of language simply because he grows up in a family that speaks a dialect other than the teacher's.[5] The dialect a child speaks indicates a good deal about his ethnic and social background; it indicates nothing at all about his intellectual potential or his current level of intellectual achievement.

Once a teacher has learned to deal with his own attitudes toward language variation, he must confront and work with the attitudes expressed by parents and school administrators. As mentioned earlier, both groups usually expect teachers to teach "good" English—that is, the English associated with the upper middle

[5] The best defense of the "legitimacy" of nonstandard dialects of English is William Labov, "The Logic of Nonstandard English," in *Language and Poverty*, ed. Frederick Williams (Chicago: Markham Publishing Co., 1970), pp. 153–90.

class. This expectation on the part of parents and administrators probably reflects, in part, their unconscious compliance with the social-class system of language that exists in this country; in most cases it also reflects a conscious acceptance of the fact that, as this society currently operates, a student's future social and economic status may depend upon his ability to speak an "acceptable" form of English.

No teacher sincerely interested in doing what is best for the students under his or her care can ignore this unfortunate fact of social life. Acceptability in this society (as currently perceived by those in control of its economic and political resources) is associated with speaking in an approved way. It is no wonder that parents, seeking the good life for their children, want them to be taught how to "talk right." Success in American universities—and in many careers—is made dependent upon the aspirant's ability to write and speak a standard form of English. Virtually all the nation's colleges and universities test the entering freshman's command of acceptable English and assign him to remedial, "bonehead" English classes if he fails the test. A serious look at most of the English proficiency tests given to college freshmen will show that many of the test items can reveal a knowledge of standard English only, so that students whose proficiency is in nonstandard English will almost certainly fail.

But forcing a student to master a second dialect of English is not without cost: as his proficiency in this new dialect increases, his ability to communicate effectively in his original dialect will probably decrease.[6] Linguistically unenlightened teachers who consider all departures from standard English mistakes that should be eradicated may view a student's conversion from nonstandard to standard English with the same sense of satisfaction missionaries have been known to exhibit over the conversion of a heathen. But no teacher aware of the regularity, beauty, and complexity of nonstandard dialects, not to mention their importance for cultural cohesion and identity, can view his complicity in their eradication without some qualms. Troubled teachers may seek comfort in the

[6] As mentioned earlier in this chapter, bidialectalism seems particularly unlikely if speaking a dialect is taken to mean commanding a range of its variant styles. For a more elaborate discussion of this issue, see Bradford Arthur, "The Interaction of Dialect and Style in Urban American English," *Language Learning* 21, no. 2 (1971): 161–73.

assumption that they are teaching standard English as a "second dialect" which can coexist with any original one; however, observation of dialect interaction and of the results of attempts to teach a second dialect casts doubt on the validity of that assumption.

Even more certainly, when a child is encouraged not to use his home dialect in situations outside the home, he begins to question the value of his original dialect and perhaps also of the cultural experiences surrounding it. Statements or insinuations from a teacher that criticize the way he speaks may lead a student to doubt himself, his family, and his friends who speak that way.

Finally, even if he is capable of mastering a second dialect without losing his first and without damaging his self-esteem, the task of doing so will still be an additional learning burden on the child who speaks an "unacceptable" dialect and virtually insures that his chance of failure in school will be greater than that of a comparable standard-English speaker. The school system expects such a student to keep up with his age group in all of the regular school subjects and to master a new dialect at the same time.

The problem facing teachers of nonstandard-English speakers in America is real and serious and inseparable from a variety of other problems associated with the nation's social divisions; simplistic half-answers will not make it disappear. Throughout linguistic history men have assigned different status labels to different languages and dialects, and past language attitudes provide this important, and perhaps encouraging, message: People are not despised simply for the way they speak; rather, speech is used as a convenient means of identifying and classifying groups of people. Because it is difficult for a man to change the dialect he speaks (just as it is difficult for him to change the color of his skin or the other physical features associated with his race), language difference is a relatively reliable indicator of group difference. If one group suspects or despises another, it transfers this attitude to the speech pattern of the alien group. Ultimately, the attitudes that the English teacher must deal with are not directed at language usage but at social groups. It seems unlikely that changing a child's dialect will fundamentally change society's attitude toward him. But if the attitude of society toward this child's culture ameliorates, or if the social group to which the child belongs gains political and economic power, then his dialect will become acceptable.

Some Advice on Teaching Standard English

Since dialect learning is natural language learning, the principles of natural language learning, described in Chapter 2, can be applied to it; one of these principles asserts that the passive mastery precedes active mastery. Accordingly, learning to understand standard English and to read it (in the sense referred to in Chapter 3 as "private" reading) should precede learning to speak, write, and read ("publicly") that same dialect. A passive knowledge of standard English is the minimum goal a teacher of standard English can set for her students. In fact, many students who speak a nonstandard dialect of English have already acquired a passive knowledge of standard English before they begin their schooling; such students have no trouble understanding the spoken equivalent of the standard English they will be asked to read during their first years of classroom education.

Determining passive mastery of standard English is especially important for teachers of children in kindergarten and the early grades, for young children are most likely to lack the exposure to standard English necessary for passive mastery. A teacher must find out at the start whether his students understand the dialect as he uses it and as it is used in textbooks and other educational materials. One technique for judging a student for passive mastery is to observe his responses to verbal commands and questions. Are his responses appropriate? Does he ask for the command or question to be repeated? Does he show other signs of confusion? A somewhat more elaborate technique might be to ask the student to act out or retell a story presented in standard English; a story cannot be acted out or retold unless it has been understood. If the student is able to respond appropriately to tasks such as these, it is reasonably certain that he understands standard English.

Inappropriate responses are more difficult to interpret. If the response requires speech from the student (an answer to a question or the retelling of a story), a failure to respond may be due to verbal shyness or a lack of active language mastery. Since active mastery is not the subject of the test, the teacher might try some of the techniques discussed in Chapter 7 for simplifying the language required of the student. Even when the appropriate response is nonverbal (obeying a command or acting out a story), a failure to respond appropriately may be caused by shyness, a hearing difficulty, a short attention span, intellectual immaturity, or any of a great number of other nonlinguistic problems.

One further word of caution is perhaps necessary. Teachers testing a student's understanding of standard English must not assume that an inability to speak standard English implies an inability to understand it. Listening to a child speak in his own dialect tells the teacher nothing about that child's passive mastery of standard English—that is, not unless the child happens to be speaking standard English. A student has understood a standard English sentence if he can paraphrase it *in his own dialect or language*.

Developing a passive knowledge of standard English in speakers of another English dialect is not an overwhelming task. Speakers of a dialect, especially young children, are able naturally to comprehend other dialects of their language simply through frequent communication with speakers of those dialects. The communication can even be one way, as in television viewing. Regularly attending a class in which standard English is spoken generally leads to a passive knowledge of the dialect.

Because a passive mastery of standard English is extremely important to functioning in a school situation where that dialect is the medium of instruction, the teacher should make every effort to facilitate such mastery in her students as rapidly and completely as possible. The classroom should be made rich in spoken standard English used in contexts where the meaning is appropriate and clear. Students need not be encouraged to speak, but they should be encouraged to respond to language: playing guessing games and participating in treasure hunts with verbal clues, acting out stories while the teacher is reading them, drawing pictures to illustrate stories, and so on. The teacher may also find it useful in the early stages to control the linguistic complexity of the standard English she uses, keeping it within the range her students understand; again, Chapter 7 suggests some techniques for language simplification.

Passive dialect mastery can be as important for teachers as it is for students; the teacher of nonstandard-English speakers may at first have difficulty understanding their dialect. Thus, since acquiring a passive knowledge of the students' dialect is a prerequisite for productive two-way verbal communication between teacher and child, teachers should open themselves to the same kinds of experiences with their students' nonstandard dialect that were discussed above in connection with providing students with a passive understanding of standard English. The teacher who accuses his students of not speaking clearly is frequently blaming them for his own inability to understand their dialect. If he were to admit his inability to understand and ask the students to help him, he would generally find them delighted over the opportunity to teach the teacher.

Assuming, then, that his nonstandard-English–speaking|students already possess or can soon acquire a passive command of standard English, the next step for a teacher of standard English is to establish priorities among the various active language skills. Since Americans are more conscious of correct usage in writing than in speech and more inclined to condemn a writer than a speaker for his dialectic shibboleths, the ability to write standard English is especially important for anyone who wishes to function effectively in the United States in matters that involve public writing. A speaker in a face-to-face oral exchange can rely on his behavior and personal appearance to help create the image he wishes to project. In written communication, the language alone represents the individual.

A mastery of a standard dialect in writing is probably easier than a mastery of the same dialect in speech. In writing, the rate of language production can be slowed down to give the individual time to compose his sentences; he can check over his work and revise any nonstandard syntax that may have slipped into his first draft. Moreover, the writer does not have to contend with the pronunciation of standard English. For these reasons teaching non-standard-English speakers to write in formal standard English would seem to be the next step following their passive mastery of the new dialect.

If writing ability is accepted as the next goal, then the problems of pronouncing words in a new way is obviated. Teachers can focus attention on mistakes that involve using incorrect syntactic features rather than incorrect pronunciations. This focus on syntax in language production seems wise even when the goal is to teach the spoken language. Differences in pronunciation are less serious blocks to social mobility than differences in syntax; most

Americans tolerate regional and ethnic variants in pronunciation as long as the syntax is standard. The natural dialects of such national figures as Presidents Kennedy and Johnson, and Martin Luther King, Jr., represent regional and ethnic pronunciations of American English that differ sharply from the national standard —that is, the pronunciation used by most radio and television announcers, for example—yet, when speaking or writing in his official role, each of these men generally used standard syntactic patterns.

Any teacher who wants to focus the students' attention on their nonstandard syntax without at the same time considering their differences in pronunciation may find that these two aspects of dialect are hard to separate without some knowledge of the grammatical rules governing the students' dialect. A classic example of the confusion of differences in pronunciation with differences in syntax can be found in the pronunciation of the past tense word ending -ed by speakers of nonstandard black English. Many educators have assumed that because speakers of this dialect frequently omit -ed from the past tense of verbs they are deficient in their grammatical knowledge of the past tense. However, a number of studies of nonstandard black English indicate that, in almost all instances, this omission of the past tense marker is controlled by a rule of pronunciation rather than a syntactic rule. Roughly speaking, this rule specifies that when a sequence of two or more consonants occurs at the end of a word or syllable, the second or last consonant is, under certain additional conditions, not pronounced. This rule causes speakers of black English to pronounce such words as *test* without the final -*t*, [tɛs], and *send* without the final -*d*, [sɛn] or [sm]. For many English verbs the past tense is signaled by the pronunciation of the second of two consonant sounds even though the presence of such a consonant sequence is not obvious from the spelling: for example, *hoped, thanked,* and *laughed* are pronounced [hopt], [θæŋkt], and [læft]. In black English, given its general rule on end-of-word pronunciation, these verbs, too, would often be pronounced without the final consonant, their only phonetic marker of the past tense. Thus a speaker of black English would probably pronounce the present and past tense of these verbs in the same way, just as they and all other speakers of English pronounce the present and past tense of the verb *put* in the same way. For those verbs whose past tense is not formed by adding another consonant onto a word that ends with a consonant (for example: *see/saw; sing/sang; bring/brought*), most speakers of black English would distinguish the pronunciation of present and past tense forms.

Since those situations in which a speaker of nonstandard English is most likely to want to use a standard dialect are formal ones and therefore require a formal style, teaching him to use formal standard English well should take precedence over teaching him to use a range of different styles within the standard dialect. In fact, since the ability to shift styles in two dialects of the same language is rarely found among speakers of English, the teacher of standard English should probably content himself with the teaching of formal standard English and accept a nonstandard form of English in less formal situations. If this approach is taken, the teaching of standard English as an active language skill becomes, for the most part, teaching the syntax of formal standard English.

Traditionally, formal standard English syntax has been taught by calling the learner's attention to instances in which his speech deviates from standard grammatical norms; he is warned, for example, against splitting infinitives or using *who* in positions requiring the objective case form. In addition, the student is taught to define and recognize marked infinitives, objects of prepositions, and direct and indirect objects of verbs—all as a prerequisite for following the grammatical rules of standard English concerning split infinitives and objective case forms. In terms used previously in this book, learning *about* the grammatical rules of standard English has traditionally been made an intermediate step in learning *how* to apply those rules to one's writing.

This traditional method of teaching the grammar of standard English seems to work reasonably well as long as its application is limited to written English. The writer has time as he composes sentences to ponder the rules he has been taught and time to proofread for any rule violations he may have missed the first time through. But most speakers, on the other hand, do not have the opportunity to revise their utterances before they are heard. And if they learned to recognize and produce standard forms by the traditional, conscious learning of rules, their speech is usually prone to inappropriate deviations from standard English.

Even when limited to written standard English, learning standard grammatical rules may be difficult for young students. For those children who entered school using a variety of English that closely approaches the written standard, the number of grammatical rules that must be juggled consciously in writing will probably not be very great. But as the number of differences between the writer's dialect and the written standard increases, the number of such rules also increases, and the task of juggling becomes more difficult. Thus, for most young students whose dialect is extensively nonstandard, the number of rules they must learn in order to convert their speech to the written standard is so great as to be overwhelming. Like their standard-speaking classmates, they are already hard pressed to master penmanship, spelling, and punctuation, not to mention the organization and communication of ideas.

An alternative to the traditional technique for teaching formal standard English might be to encourage students to learn this form of English as an extension of their natural language learning. The student would be encouraged to use formal standard variants in his own writing only after he had demonstrated that he could recognize these variants and distinguish them from nonstandard grammatical variants. That is, his recognition of standard English would precede any insistence that he produce it. Moreover, his capacity to produce standard English would be allowed to proceed in a gradual fashion; early lapses into an inappropriate syntax would not be criticized. Instead of offering discouragement, the teacher would rely on the writer's capacity for self-correction and on his unconscious knowledge of the differences between varieties of English. At most the teacher might ask the writer to reconsider what he had written, and perhaps to try phrasing it in a more formal way or in imitation of some individual known to the writer who uses formal standard English. Similarly, following this natural language-learning procedure for teaching formal standard English, the writer would be encouraged to use standard English fluently and naturally without consciously understanding the grammatical rules he is following; his ability to do so would be based upon an unconscious assimilation of these rules without prior explanations. Again, in terms defined earlier in this text, knowing *how* to produce formal standard English does not require any previous knowledge *about* that particular variety of English.

Reading, Writing, and Standard English

Some teachers assume that their students must learn standard English as a prerequisite to learning how to read and write English. This is only partly true. For reading especially, the importance of knowing standard English is frequently exaggerated. The reader needs only a passive knowledge of the dialect used in the text he is reading; since most English-language books are written in the standard dialect, a passive knowledge of standard English is required for reading them. However, as was mentioned earlier, this knowledge is easily and naturally acquired by any English-speaking student, even if he or she is very young.

Certainly a student does not have to be able to use a standard pronunciation in order to read standard English. The only valid requirement is that he recognize the written word as corresponding to or representing a known unit of meaning in the language. And this is true whether he is reading silently to himself or delivering a recitation. Nonetheless, many teachers of reading constantly correct a child's pronunciation of a word until it is replaced by the standard pronunciation. This is as foolish as correcting a speaker of standard American English when he reads aloud from a British author without using a British accent. If, in reading standard English, a child pronounces a word as it is normally pronounced in his own English dialect, then he has read that word correctly.

A child has learned how to write when he knows how to express his own dialect in alphabetic symbols. Learning a new dialect as a form of communication that can be expressed in writing is an entirely different and more complicated task. Teachers must, therefore, be able to distinguish errors that indicate a child has not learned to express his own dialect in writing from errors that indicate he has not learned another dialect of his language. Finally, a teacher of spelling must recognize that the ability to spell a word does not depend upon the ability to pronounce it in a certain way. There is no need for a speaker of nonstandard English to learn standard pronunciation as a prerequisite for spelling.

An English teacher can begin to consider the true effects of dialect on reading or composition only when she can separate learning how to read or write from learning a second dialect of English. Once this distinction is clear, it also becomes clear that regardless of which English dialect a child speaks—standard or nonstandard; northern, midlands, or southern; British or American —literacy in the language requires an association between *that* dialect and written symbols.

However, since learning how to read and write depends on the ability to relate a set of visual alphabetic symbols to a known language system, it follows that some characteristics of nonstandard dialects will, to some extent, affect their speakers' association of the language with its written representation. These characteristics are the subject of the next chapter.

EFFECTS OF DIALECT DIFFERENCE IN READING AND WRITING

In earlier chapters on the linguistics of reading and writing, it was assumed that the learner of these skills spoke the dialect used by his teachers and reading texts. Thus, he was expected to expand his vocabulary and range of styles, but not expected to alter his dialect in any more fundamental way. For this type of student, learning how to read and write is principally a matter of associating a new set of symbols with a known language system. For those learners whose dialect is not the same as their teachers' and textbooks', however, additional problems arise.

Since all the children in a community speak a somewhat different version of English than its adults, few young students use a dialect that is identical to their teachers'; however, the difference is generally minor and does not interfere seriously with classroom instruction. More serious learning problems are likely to confront students whose dialect represents the speech of lower socioeconomic groups or of ethnic minorities. And, since a disproportionately large number of ethnic-minority-group students are in the lower socioeconomic groups, the chances that they will have such dialect differences are exceedingly high.

Indeed, the special reading problems that face ethnic-minority-group students are of more than theoretical interest. With tragic frequency these students reach the end of their elementary, and sometimes their secondary-school, education without ever learning how to read or write. Recent reading-test scores for all sixth-grade students in the Los Angeles public schools confirm this tendency. The chart on the opposite page compares reading achievement scores for sixth-graders in two groups of elementary schools within the Los Angeles school system. The first group comprises all of those schools with at least 80 percent "Anglo" students—that is, Caucasian students of European ancestry. The other group comprises all those schools with 80 percent ethnic-minority students; most of these minority-group students are from either black or Mexican-American families. As this chart indicates, Anglo students in the Los Angeles area succeed in learning how to read; their median score is slightly above the national median. But the range of reading achievement among minority schools scarcely overlaps the range for the Anglo schools. The median score for this second group is between the tenth and twentieth percentile—more than 30 percent below the national median. The Los Angeles school system has recognized for several years its failure to teach reading successfully to minority-group students. Time, money, and expertise have been invested in attempts to improve the level of minority-group reading instruction; thus, the failure here cannot be attributed primarily to neglect.

The Los Angeles school system has not made a similar interschool test of composition skills—or, at any rate, has not publicly announced the results of one. Since reading is normally a prerequisite for writing (passive skills precede active skills), one can only imagine that the need for improvement in composition in minority schools is also at the point of a crisis. Anecdotal evidence from individual English teachers supports this grim view. When, as is the case in many large high schools, students are assigned different English classes according to their achievement levels, the lowest-level classes consistently contain the highest percentages of minority-group students. Vast numbers of young Americans living in inner-city areas are emerging from the schools functionally illiterate.

Unquestionably, inner-city schools have problems; but what are the causes of those problems and to what extent are they linguistic? One cause is undoubtedly American attitudes toward minority cultures. The inner-city student's poor learning is due in

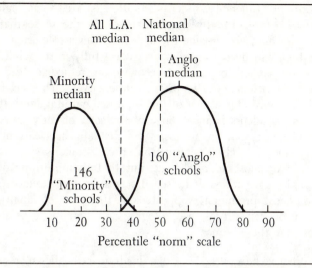

READING LEVELS OF LOS ANGELES SIXTH-GRADERS

All L.A. median
National median
Anglo median
Minority median
146 "Minority" schools
160 "Anglo" schools

10 20 30 40 50 60 70 80 90
Percentile "norm" scale

part to the prejudice and apathy of the school system and to the alienation and tension among the students, all of which reflects the cultural tensions within the United States. The failure of American society to acknowledge its black, brown, red, and yellow citizens is reflected in its failure to teach their history as part of American history, to teach their literature as part of American literature, and to accept their language as legitimate for school use. The establishment of ethnic-studies programs within the schools, the initiation of bilingual education, the hiring of teachers who understand and respect the backgrounds of their students, the questioning of tests that may be culturally biased or of admissions requirements that may exclude minority students from colleges and universities—all these are belated attempts to adjust the curriculum and the schools to meet the needs of all the students. Such adjustments should be linguistically oriented to the extent that social attitudes create and are perpetuated in attitudes toward language and dialect.

Many educators have attributed part of the failure of minority-group students to deficiencies existing in the students' cultural background. Inner-city students are often referred to as "culturally deprived" or "culturally disadvantaged" in the sense that their home life does not provide them with the level of cultural experience they will need to participate successfully in school. This explanation has led to the creation of various remedial Head Start–type programs in order to prepare inner-city preschoolers for the public schools. One aspect of this supposed cultural deprivation of inner-city students is an absence of the sorts of early experiences with language that are necessary for first-language learning. This theory does not claim simply that these students speak a non-standard or substandard dialect, but that their learning of their first dialect, regardless of its social status, has been retarded. One of the most prominent supporters of this view of language deficiency or deprivation, psychologist Carl Bereiter, expresses the problem in these terms:

> We have heard it said . . . that disadvantaged children are not culturally deprived but only culturally different, and that there are intelligent and capable children in every disadvantaged group. Charitable as these comments may be, they nevertheless serve to divert our attention from the fundamental problems. . . . By the time they are five years old, disadvantaged children of almost every kind are typically one to two years retarded in language development. . . . Half a century of studies on the prediction of school success clearly establishes that verbal abilities are the best single predicators of achievement in a wide variety of school subjects. Thus the child who enters school markedly behind in the development of verbal abilities enters with a severe handicap.[1]

Linguists have shown little sympathy for this theory of language deprivation. Most contend that the child raised in a minority culture is not therefore deprived of culture and that, similarly, the child who speaks a nonstandard dialect of English is not by that fact deprived of language. Indeed, some of the evidence that supposedly indicates poor verbal abilities in English actually indicates the successful learning of one of its nonstandard dialects. Psychologists only partially aware of a child's dialect may mistake his

---

[1] "Academic Instruction and Preschool Children," in *Language Programs for the Disadvantaged*, ed. Richard Corbin and Muriel Crosby (Champaign, Ill.: National Council of Teachers of English, 1965), pp. 195–97.

dialect differences for grammatical errors and attribute them to low aptitude or a home environment devoid of coherent speech. They may not realize, for instance, that in black English, *That baby sleepy* is both grammatical and complete.

In their analyses of the speech of young inner-city children, psychologists have exhibited other forms of linguistic naïveté as well. For example, they have asserted that the use of incomplete sentences is an indication of a failure at language learning—that it indicates an inability to produce complete sentences, which are assumed more difficult. From a linguist's point of view, however, the order of difficulty is totally reversed, since the rules describing the structure of grammatical incomplete sentences (not all incomplete sentences are grammatical)[2] must be based on a structural description of the corresponding complete sentence. In forming such grammatical sentence fragments, the speaker must apply certain "reduction rules" to the complete-sentence structure. Thus, the child who says, "Under the table," rather than, "The book is under the table," in reply to the question, "Where is the book?" is demonstrating a higher rather than a lower level of language mastery. Many linguists question the discouraging psychological analyses of language learning among inner-city children on methodological grounds as well as on conceptual ones. They point out that a child is often reluctant to speak in situations he or she considers threatening and that, especially for a young inner-city child, such situations generally include encounters with psychologists, linguists, or teachers. The inner-city child who demonstrates little language learning during formal speech tests has often proved amply and even abundantly verbal, when placed in what he feels is a less threatening situation.

Many other ethnic-minority children within America's schools are supposed to have language difficulties not because they speak a nonstandard variety of English but because they speak a language other than English. Spanish-speaking children from the Puerto

[2] For example, in response to a question like *Where will you be staying?* a speaker of English might use the grammatical complete sentence
I'll be staying at my folks' place,
or a grammatical incomplete sentence such as
At my folks' place,
but never the ungrammatical incomplete sentence
*Staying at my folks' place.

Rican sections of New York City, the Mexican-American barrios of Los Angeles, or the communities of migrant Mexican-American farmworkers throughout the Southwest; young residents of New York's or San Francisco's Chinatown who speak Cantonese; the children on Indian reservations near Gallup, New Mexico, who speak Navajo—are all generally included in this category. For some of these students English is, indeed, a strange new language which they encounter for the first time in school. Ideally, teachers of such students should have training in the special techniques for teaching English as a second language, most of which are outside the scope of this book. The teacher of non-English speakers who has not received this training must rely heavily on the students' own natural language-learning ability and use techniques for lan-.guage simplification such as those suggested in Chapter 7.

One should not naïvely assume, however, as many educators have, that all children from neighborhoods populated primarily by non-English speakers will necessarily, or even generally, be unable to speak English when they reach school age. In a surprisingly large number of cases, this assumption would prove false. Many students from non–English-speaking neighborhoods are native speakers of English—in a nonstandard dialect strongly influenced by some other language. For example, many children with Spanish surnames in the Los Angeles area do not speak Spanish fluently, even though they come from a Mexican-American ghetto area and usually pronounce English words in much the same way they would be pronounced by a native speaker of Spanish. Similar sorts of nonstandard dialects of English have been observed in the city's Chinese community and on Indian reservations. No teacher should assume that a student is not a native speaker of English simply because that student has a foreign surname or speaks English with what sounds like a foreign accent. And if he is a native speaker of English, he does not need a course in speaking English before he can learn to read and write it, but merely a teacher who understands how to teach these skills to speakers of nonstandard dialects.

Beyond the problems created by cultural attitudes, possible cultural disadvantage, and bilingualism, there remains the possibility that the reading difficulties of many students may be due in part to the more immediate effects of inappropriate teaching methods and materials. Several specific linguistic problems related to teaching techniques warrant detailed consideration in the remainder of this chapter.

Reading: Word Recognition

One of the skills an individual needs for reading is the ability to associate a series of written letters with a word in his or her oral vocabuary.[3] Among the strategies for word recognition suggested in Chapter 3, only the whole-word recognition strategies are not affected by dialect differences. All those that require matching letters with sounds or looking for phonic clues within the spelling of words will be affected by such differences. For instance, a beginning reader who speaks a dialect in which the sound [l] does not occur at the end of words, so that words like *go* and *goal* are homophones, will need a special "sounding-out" rule stating that the spelling *l* or *ll* at the end of words is silent. If this child were to follow the regular rule for sounding out *l* or *ll*, he would produce sequences of sounds that did not represent words in his dialect. He is not likely to find the silent-*l* rule in his spelling manuals, and most teachers and reading tests would encourage him to sound out the letter *l* unless it is silent in the standard dialect— as in *calm* and *palm*, for example—thus inhibiting his recognition of many words with that spelling.

For many speakers of a nonstandard dialect of English this problem with sounding out words is only a pseudoproblem, since they recognize and use both standard pronunciation variants and nonstandard pronunciation variants. The example in the preceding paragraph assumes that the nonstandard-English speaker *always* drops the [l] sound at the end of words. Current evidence suggests that most if not all of the rules distinguishing nonstandard pronunciation from standard pronunciation, including the silent-*l* rule, are optional. Many speakers of nonstandard English—almost all the evidence is based on nonstandard northern urban black English—use the standard pronunciation as well as one or more nonstandard pronunciations for most of the words in their vocabu-

---

[3] This skill is different from vocabulary enrichment, which involves increasing the number of words the reader knows rather than the number he knows how to read.

lary. Consequently, even when they are taught rules for sounding out that associate each letter with its standard pronunciations, these nonstandard dialect speakers can generally arrive at one of the pronunciations possible in their dialect.

Even if the reader does not have the standard pronunciation as an option in his own speech, sounding out words by standard rules raises problems only if the reader cannot recognize the standard pronunciation. Reading is after all a passive, recognition skill. Many speakers of nonstandard English, because of their extensive exposure to standard English through the mass media and elsewhere, are able to recognize a word from its standard pronunciation. Thus, difficulties with sounding out words are not inevitable for speakers of nonstandard English even if the rules for the process produce pronunciations they do not normally use.

But if a reader is unable to recognize words from their standard pronunciations, standard procedures for sounding them out are useless, and some alternative method must be employed. At least two such approaches are possible. New rules for sounding out words can be written to represent the correspondence between standard spelling and the pronunciation of words in the reader's dialect. For nonstandard black English one of the new rules might read as follows: the letter *t* at the end of a word is silent when it follows the letter *s* (*rest, past, cost*) or the letter *n* (*sent, mint, want*). Another way of stating this same rule would be to say that the sequences *st* and *nt* at the end of words are digraph spellings for the sounds [s] and [n] in the same way that *th* and *ph* are digraph spellings. Another sounding-out rule for black English might be: the spelling *th* is pronounced either [t] or [d] when it occurs before vowels, and either [f] or [v] when it occurs after vowels. Following this rule the spelling *thin* would be sounded out [tɪn] and the spelling *path* would be sounded out [pæf].

Some teachers have considered another approach for readers unable to recognize words from their standard pronunciation: the spelling of English words can be changed so that by following the usual "sounding-out" rules, a reader arrives at the nonstandard pronunciation. New rules such as those in the preceding paragraph would be unnecessary, but the words affected—such as the words *rest, past, cost, sent, mint, want, thin,* and *path*—would be re-spelled: *res, pas, cos, sen, min, wan, tin,* and *paf.* This procedure is generally followed in popular literature that makes use of nonstandard dialects. For instance, in *Huckleberry Finn*, Mark Twain represented the speech of the black slave, Jim, in the following way:

> Dey's two gals flyin' 'bout you in yo' life. One uv 'em's light en t'other one is dark. One is rich en t'other is po'. You's gwyne to marry de po' one fust en de rich one by en by.[4]

However, the value of using this sort of respelling in reading primers designed for speakers of various nonstandard dialects is highly questionable. For one thing, all English-speaking children should eventually learn to deal with standard English spelling since nearly all the reading material they will confront as adults will employ the accepted spelling system. Moreover, although respelling words makes sounding them out easier, other word-recognition techniques, such as recognition of whole-word shape, would be hindered if the reader's exposure to the shape of words in normal English spelling were delayed.[5]

The emphasis on sounding out misses the important interaction between this reading strategy and other methods of word recognition. Unless the word to be read occurs in total isolation from any verbal or nonverbal context clues, the reader who knows it in its oral form need not rely solely on sounding out when attempting to identify it. If a reader is aware of the context of an unrecognized word, he can usually guess its identity with fair accuracy. The part context plays in word identification was illustrated in Chapter 3 in connection with the word *penguin* in the sentence *The penguin waddled slowly*. Obviously, in this case the word in question, *penguin*, can only be the name of some class of things that can waddle slowly. That class, however, is fairly large. But once the reader has gotten that far, he can use sounding out as a supplementary strategy. If he considers only the first letter of the word, he can assume that the name of the waddler begins with the sound [p]. If, in addition, he looks at the last letter he gains the further clue that the name ends with the sound [n]. Perhaps

---

[4] *Huckleberry Finn*, chapter 4.

[5] The Initial Teaching Alphabet (ITA) is a widely known attempt to modify English spelling in reading primers so that spelling represents pronunciation in a systematic way. The special alphabetic symbols used in the ITA each represent only one sound and are carefully designed to distort as little as possible the shape of the word as normally spelled.

as a third step in this partial reliance on sounding out, the reader might note that the word contains two vowel nuclei and that, therefore, it is probably two syllables long. Even if he is limited to these three rather simple phonic clues, the reader can drastically narrow the range of possible identities for the unknown word. In most cases this amount of sounding out would be more than sufficient for precise identification of the word.

This partial use of sounding out is an especially important skill for readers of English, since in English it is rarely possible to state simple rules for associating every letter in a word with a sound. The vowels of English are notoriously difficult to sound out, and most readers probably rely primarily on consonants for phonic clues. For speakers of standard English, the spelling of a consonant preceded in a word or syllable by a vowel generally corresponds to a sound in the pronunciation of that word or syllable. These post-vocalic consonants are less likely to be pronounced in such non-standard dialects as black English, however. Thus, those teaching reading to speakers of that dialect must know when it leaves post-vocalic consonant spellings unpronounced, and therefore relatively useless as sources of phonic clues for word identification. Also, since the prevocalic consonant spellings provide excellent phonic clues for word identification in this dialect, its speakers should be taught to make maximum use of these letters in sounding out un-recognized words.

Some of the morphemic endings that occur in English spelling are generally unpronounced in black English; these include the -ed used for the past tense and the -s used for the possessive and plural of nouns and for the third person, singular, present tense indicative of verbs. The fact that speakers of black English may not always pronounce markers of possession, plurality, or the past tense in no way indicates that they lack these semantic concepts. It should be noted, however, that, for the reader who does not pronounce them in his speech, the spellings -ed and -s at the end of verbs and nouns have no phonic value, even though they stand for semantic units that he can recognize and use in understanding total sentence meaning. It might therefore be wise for a teacher to encourage such readers in their tendency to regard these endings as signals of meaning without independent phonic value, just as he encourages all his students to attend to quotation marks or question marks as conveyors of meaning that are not themselves pronounced.[6] The teacher could explain that the -s at the end of a noun means that the noun refers to more than one thing or person without insisting that the -s be pronounced.

Reading: Comprehension of Syntax

In order to read, students must understand not only the meaning of individual words but the meaning of sentences and paragraphs. To the extent that the sentence structures used in the student's dialect differ from those used in the reading material, there is a possibility that the student will be unable to understand the sentences he reads even though he understands all the individual words in those sentences. Again, as with word recognition, this may be for many or even most students only a pseudoproblem, since syntactic comprehension requires only a passive mastery of whatever unfamiliar sentence structures are used in the reading materials. The problem such children face is comparable with the problem any American faces in reading the works of English or Australian authors, or for that matter the problems that a northerner faces in reading a novel by William Faulkner.

But by the same token, it is unquestionably easier to read a familiar dialect than an unfamiliar one, and of course any reader is most familiar with his own dialect. Some linguists and educators have therefore suggested that beginning reading texts for speakers of a nonstandard dialect be written in the readers' own dialect. A few such dialect texts have been written for nonstandard black English; they retain standard spelling, but the ordering of words, the choice of words, and the occurrence of inflectional endings represent the syntactic patterns occurring within the nonstandard dialect and the vocabulary most often used by its speakers. In the

---

[6] Since a question demanding a yes or no response (see pp. 133–34) is frequently pronounced with a rising intonation at the end, its question mark might be said to be "pronounced." Other types of questions, however, end with the same intonation as statements.

following example, the same poem is represented first in a standard version and then in a nonstandard version.[7]

SEE A GIRL

Standard English Version	Black English Version
"Look down here," said Suzy. "I can see a girl in here. That girl looks like me. Come here and look, David. Can you see that girl?"	Susan say, "Hey you-all, look down here. I can see a girl in here. The girl, she look like me. Come here and look, David. Could you see the girl?"
"Here I come," said David. "I want to see the girl." David said, "I do not see a girl. A girl is not in here, Suzy. I see me and my ball."	David, he say, "Here I come. Let me see the girl." David say, "I don't see no girl. Ain't no girl in there. I see me and my ball."
Suzy said, "Look in here, Mother. David can not see a girl And I can. Can you see a girl in here?"	Susan, she say, "Momma, look in here. David don't see no girl, and I do. You see a girl in there?"
"Look down, Suzy," said Mother. "Look down here, David. That little girl is my Suzy. And here is David."	Momma say, "Look down there, David. That little girl Susan. And there go David."
"Mother! Mother!" said Suzy. "We can see David and me. We can see Wiggles and a big girl. That big girl is you."	Susan say, "Momma! Momma! We can see David and me. We can see Wiggles and a big girl. You that big girl."

[7] The setting of this story involves a little girl who looks at her reflection in a puddle. Wiggles is a dog. Both versions of the poem appear in Walter A. Wolfram and Ralph W. Fasold, "Towards Reading Materials for Speakers of Black English: Three Linguistically Appropriate Passages," in *Teaching Black Children to Read*, ed. Joan C. Baratz and Roger W. Shy (Washington, D.C.: Center for Applied Linguistics, 1969), pp. 147–49.

Proponents of dialect texts have argued that these texts are desirable for nonlinguistic reasons as well as linguistic ones. They maintain that a child may gain respect for himself and his culture by seeing his form of English used in writing. This use of dialect texts prevents speakers of nonstandard dialects from getting the impression that their dialects cannot be, or are not worthy of being, written down.

A related but less drastic departure from standard reading texts would be texts that use standard English but avoid constructions and vocabulary items that differ drastically from those found in the nonstandard dialect spoken by the student. The language of the text would be drawn from the subpart of standard English that is shared by the nonstandard dialect. Such a text intended for use by speakers of black English would, for example, use direct discourse in which black and standard English share similar grammatical structures and would avoid indirect discourse in which the syntax of black English differs markedly from the standard dialect. The child who speaks black English could understand without difficulty a passage like *Wilber wondered, should he go or shouldn't he;* but that same child might have difficulty understanding *Wilber wondered whether or not he should go,* since in black English indirect questions are not formed by using *whether.*

Public Reading for Dialect Speakers

Those who teach reading to speakers of a nonstandard dialect must recognize that dialect differences have differing effects on private reading than they do on public reading. Since private reading requires only the passive ability to comprehend the meaning of the written text (see Chapter 3), it is seldom seriously hindered by dialect differences. On the other hand, public reading, which requires of the reader a fluent, oral rendition of the text, is drastically impeded when the dialect the reader must reproduce varies significantly from his own. But as long as the text avoids constructions that are not present in his dialect, or as long as he is allowed to use his own dialect in delivering oral readings of works written in the standard dialect, the nonstandard-dialect speaker need not experience dialect-related reading problems. For public reading, certainly, the dialect reading texts described above are highly desirable.

Unfortunately, many teachers of reading fail to recognize the difference between the demands of private and public reading: in teaching reading comprehension (private reading), they insist that each of their students be able to give a public standard-English rendition of his reading text. This places an inordinate additional learning burden on readers who are speakers of nonstandard dialects. Many of the "errors" that such readers make and that teachers insist be corrected are in fact pseudoerrors, and they indicate an understanding of the reading material rather than confusion. When a reader pronounces a word as it is normally pronounced in his own dialect, he shows that he has recognized and understood that word. A black student's failure to read the past tense -ed or the plural -s does not necessarily mean that he has ignored these markers; quite possibly, he has understood their part in the meaning of the sentence but, in rendering that sentence in his dialect, generally omits them. This sort of explanation is also possible for "errors" involving the substitution of multiple negation for single negation or a choice between other such grammatical alternatives. It is completely natural, inevitable, and desirable for a reader to convert the syntactic structures of his reading matter into the equivalent structures used in his dialect; all readers do it to some extent.

A teacher's insistence on a public reading in standard English may have dire consequences for a student who speaks nonstandard English. The reader may be forced to focus on each word individually in order to achieve the acceptable pronunciations and to make sure that no words are changed or omitted. This forced attention to individual words—more specifically, to the pronunciation of those words—may prevent the reader from attending to their meanings and the meanings of the sentences in which they occur. He may literally train himself to ignore sentence meaning as a strategy for avoiding "mistakes." Frequently speakers of nonstandard English remain what reading teachers call "word readers," very carefully pronouncing one word at a time but failing to pronounce or to recognize phrases and sentences; such students score low on reading comprehension tests.

Dialect Difference and Writing

Since writing is an active language skill, the composition teacher can expect to encounter confusion and difficulty when he asks students to produce compositions in a dialect other than their own. The following theme, written by a ninth-grade student in Los Angeles who is a speaker of black English, illustrates the sorts of difficulty that an inner-city composition teacher encounters.

ROOM 292

Room 292 is a that as not taugh me to much. It is a ugly room it is set up like this: the teacher desk on the east wall in front of the chalk board the chalk board is on a blue-green wall, the north wall is a off-yellow on it is a green chalk board on the chalk board are the words "Do Not Erase" "Important Dates To Remember" and so on, on the west wall which a off-green are papers and on the board in big black letters are "POTPOURRI," on the south are a rolls of window, and in the middle of it all 35 chairs and in the chairs are students. This room is not teachering me anything.
The End

Faced with a composition such as this one, the teacher may wonder how best to help the writer improve his composition skills. Marking errors with a red pencil is obviously not enough.

Perhaps a better way to start is by determining the extent to which the difficulties the student is having are caused by dialect differences. On first reading, the teacher may wonder whether this student can, in fact, produce English that is grammatical in any dialect. One way to answer this question is to try supplying the punctuation that is missing in the paper. If the theme can be divided into grammatical sentences, then presumably the student can produce such sentences, even though he cannot properly indicate their boundaries in writing. Following this procedure, the above theme might be divided as follows:

*   1. Room 292 is a that as not taugh me to much.
      2. It is a ugly room.
      3. It is set up like this:
*?   4. The teacher desk on the east wall in front of the chalk board.
      5. The chalk board is on a blue-green wall.

6. The north wall is a off-yellow.
7. On it is a green chalk board.
8. On the chalk board are the words "<u>Do Not Erase</u>" "<u>Important Dates to Remember</u>" and so on.
* 9. On the west wall which a off-green are papers.
10. And on the board in big black letters are "POT-POURRI."
11. On the south are a rolls of window.
*? 12. And in the middle of it all 35 chairs.
13. And in the chairs are students.
14. This room is not teachering me anything.

Only four of these "sentences" are deficient in the sense that they appear to lack a word necessary for completeness. Sentence 1 lacks a noun after the article *a*, and sentences 4, 9, and 12 lack a form of the verb *to be*. (Sentences 4 and 12 are conceivably grammatical even without this verb.)

The missing noun in sentence 1 seems to be a result of carelessness on the part of the writer. No rule of black English would lead to the omission of a word in this position. Confronted with this sentence, the writer would probably recognize his mistake and put in a noun such as *place* or *room*. The omission of the verb *to be*, on the other hand, is a well-documented characteristic of the writer's dialect, and is discussed in more detail below. It is sufficient to note here that none of these mistakes indicates that the writer does not know how to use English.

Two other mistakes in this composition are conceivably the result of carelessness or of confusion that is not related to dialect interference. The use of the plural form *are* in sentence 10 where the singular is called for may be either a careless carrying over of the plurality indicated by the preceding noun *letters* or a sign of confusion as to the number of the noun *potpourri*, an uncommon noun in anyone's dialect. Similarly, the word *teachering* in the last sentence may be the result of inadvertently writing *teacher* rather than *teach* before adding the *-ing*. (That the writer was clearly able to use the verb *to teach* is shown in his use of the past tense of that verb in sentence 1.) Also, *teachering* might conceivably be a word peculiar to the writer's dialect, or perhaps the writer has intentionally created a word. Without further evidence, it is impossible to say for sure.

Other "errors," however, are clearly caused by the writer's use of a nonstandard dialect. Most of the spelling errors are of this sort.

In sentence 1 the writer confuses the spelling of the word *to* with that of the word *too* because in his dialect, as in every other dialect of English, these two words are pronounced in the same way. In that same sentence the lack of a final *t* on *taught* and of an initial *h* on *has* is almost certainly a reflection of the fact that in the writer's dialect neither letter is consistently sounded in those words. As long as spelling is based on or related to pronunciation, spellers will fail to include letters they do not pronounce and will confuse the spelling of words they pronounce in the same way; this is not a special characteristic of writers who speak a non-standard dialect. What is special about a speaker of nonstandard English is the particular sets of words he pronounces the same and the particular letters he fails to pronounce. These two factors are related in that it is precisely the omission or changing of sounds within a word which creates new homophones.

Words pronounced differently in one dialect but the same way in another are more likely to create confusion for the speller who speaks the dialect in which they are pronounced identically. The fact that such confusion can occur does not mean, however, that homophonic pairs of words are somehow wrong; all languages and all dialects contain homophones. Nor does it mean that all speakers of a language should be taught to pronounce words in a single (standard) manner—even if such a proposal were possible, the cost in teacher and student man-hours would be vastly out of proportion to any conceivable benefits for spelling. But homophones do create spelling problems, and dialects differ as to which pairs of words are homophones. These two facts suggest that speakers of different dialects will face different problems in learning how to spell. Spelling teachers and writers of spelling workbooks should be aware of these differences and should tailor their instruction to the dialect of the student.

Returning to the student's theme, several additional errors can be attributed to differences between the rules describing the writer's dialect and those describing standard English. The writer consistently uses the article *a* before vowel sounds. In standard English the variant *an* is required in such instances; in the writer's dialect two vowels can occur without an intervening consonant. In sentence 4 the absence of the possessive marker *'s* on the noun *teacher* is due to the fact that the writer's dialect does not mark the possessive when the noun representing the possessor comes before the noun representing the thing possessed. In black English this possessive marker occurs only when the possessor noun is in the predicate of the sentence: *That desk is the teacher's.*

Finally, as was noted earlier, the omission of the verb *to be* in sentences 4, 9, and 12 is a phonological characteristic of black English. This deletion appears to be governed by a rule similar to the rule which leads to the contraction of the verb *to be* in other dialects of English. In black English this contraction can be carried one step further to the complete deletion of the verb. Note that in all cases where the verb is deleted it could have been, and in all but the most formal speech would have been, contracted in standard English.

Based on observations of dialect interference such as these, the teacher might conclude that the writer of "Room 292" has simply used his own dialect rather than standard English. This conclusion would be an oversimplification, however: the writer was probably trying to use a dialect other than his own, but was only partially successful. The places where the writer has failed to repress his nonstandard dialect would be obvious to most speakers of standard English, but his successes and partial success would be hard for such speakers to recognize unless they had studied the grammatical rules of his dialect. In fact, it is impossible to document this kind of success with absolute certainty because it is always possible that in using a standard grammatical form the speaker of a nonstandard dialect is merely inadvertently choosing one of the options offered in his own dialect. Nonetheless, the instances in which the author of "Room 292" has used forms that are not typical of his dialect are worthy of note. Though many speakers of black English do not pronounce the *-s* on plural nouns, this writer has consistently included the plural *-s* wherever standard English would consider it necessary—with the possible exception of the word *window*, for which the plural seems to have been transferred to an earlier noun. In addition, a form of the verb *to be* was included in all but three of the sentences in which a speaker of standard English would use one, and only in sentence 10 was that form not the one standard English considers appropriate. Certainly the negation that occurs in the last sentence is entirely standard: it follows the rules for single negation rather than the rules for multiple negation described in Chapter 5. Although several times in the composition the writer omits letters that are not pronounced in his dialect, in many more cases he includes such letters. To consider only one example, the word *board* would be pronounced by this writer without sounding the *r*. Yet this word is consistently spelled correctly.

Among the misspellings in "Room 292," the use of the sequence *rolls* for the word *row* is of special interest because it provides positive evidence that the writer is trying to represent a dialect foreign to his own. The writer certainly did not include the *ll* at the end of this word because he pronounces the word *row* with a final [l] sound; in fact, he probably pronounces both the words *row* and *roll* in the same way, that is, without a final consonant. His misspelling of *row* shows that he realizes that in some cases silent letters *ll* must be represented in order to make a spelling correct. His addition of such silent letters where they do not belong is an example not of his failure to correct but of overcorrection. This would never occur if the writer were simply trying to represent his own dialect.

A thorough analysis of the errors summarized in the preceding paragraphs requires a recognition of the special characteristics of the student's nonstandard dialect and of the differences between that dialect and the dialect used in the school. A teacher with this knowledge can categorize the language-related problems a student faces in writing compositions, and then treat each group of problems in an appropriate way. In the preceding analysis, for example, problems of punctuation and of careless word omission were distinguishable from problems related to dialect modification. A linguistically sophisticated composition teacher would isolate and focus the writer's attention on instances of careless omission and then tackle the most easily corrected instances of dialect difficulty —for example, the exclusion of the indefinite article *an*. He could move from there to extremely difficult dialect-related errors, such as the omission of the verb *to be* at points in the sentence where this verb cannot be omitted in the standard dialect.

The teacher of composition who has a good knowledge of dialects can use it to gauge the progress his students are making at learning to write. In correcting students' papers, he will be as concerned with the dialect differences that have been successfully recognized and represented as he is with the unrecognized differences that show up as errors.

RECOGNIZING AND CONTROLLING SENTENCE DIFFICULTY

Teachers, whether of English or of some other subject, may need to estimate the difficulty of the language used in school textbooks and, where indicated, make that language easier for their students to understand and respond to. This need is obvious for teachers of students encountering English for the first time; but language simplification should concern all teachers to some extent, since difficult language adds to the burden any learner must bear and may contribute to a breakdown of his ability or will to learn.

For most students language experience in school is primarily passive—the student reads or listens, and his task is to understand. But a student's linguistic participation in class cannot remain entirely passive. He must at the very least be able to answer questions put to him by the teacher. The first two sections of this chapter discuss some of the ways in which words and sentence structures can be difficult for students to understand, and make suggestions as to how such difficulties can be overcome; the third section describes some causes of and cures for the difficulties students may have in answering questions.

Recognizing and Simplifying Difficult Vocabulary

A sentence is most likely to be difficult to understand because some of the words it contains are difficult to understand. But what makes words difficult to understand? First, words are difficult when the object or concept they refer to is unfamiliar, complicated, or confusing. Such words as *democracy, phoneme, God,* and *electrostatic* are, for many students, difficult in this way. This is not to say that these words themselves are unfamiliar; *democracy* and *God* are within the vocabulary of most speakers of English. But different people mean different things when they use these words, and most people would have considerable difficulty if asked to explain them. God is viewed as personal, three-personal, and impersonal—a Heavenly Father or the ground of all being.

Second, words are difficult when they are unfamiliar, even though what they refer to is familiar. In most cases, they are unfamiliar because their association with some object or concept is unfamiliar. For example, most of us, through movies and book illustrations, are familiar with the appearance of a suit of medieval armor; but few of us could identify the *palette,* the *cuisse,* or the *tasset.* These three terms are likely to be unfamiliar even to the person who can recognize the objects to which they refer: the armor plates that protect the shoulder, thigh, and hip. In other cases, words are unfamiliar because of the context in which they occur; that is, because their grammatical function in the particular sentence is not their usual one. Consider the sentence *The unmusical plague the community sings*: in it *unmusical,* normally an adjective, is used as a noun; *plague,* normally a noun, is used as a verb; *community,* normally a noun, is used as an adjective;[1] and *sings,* normally a verb, is used as a noun. Finally, words may be unfamiliar if they are pronounced in an unfamiliar way. A noted American linguist, Leonard Bloomfield, describes an encounter with a London cabby: "A London cabman did not understand me when I asked to be driven to the *Comedy Theatre*: I had

---

[1] Even though the word *community* is used here as an adjective—that is, to modify a noun—it does not share with attributive adjectives the capacity to bear modification or qualification designating comparative or superlative degree —as, for example, with the use of the inflections -*er* and -*est.* Thus, *community* here is not, strictly speaking, an adjective.

forgotten myself and spoken the American form of the first vowel in *comedy*, and this the Englishman could take only as a representative of the vowel phoneme in a word like *car*—so that I was really asking for a *Carmody Theatre*, which does not exist."[2]

Difficult words make sentences, paragraphs, and larger linguistic units difficult to understand insofar as an understanding of these words is prerequisite to an understanding of the larger unit. To determine the degree to which not knowing the meaning of a word or group of words precludes understanding the meaning of the sentence in which they occur, remove the words in question from the sentence. If the meaning of the sentence remains pretty much intact, or if the meaning of the missing words can be easily guessed from the context (which may include pictures and diagrams as well as other words and sentences), then, regardless of their difficulty, the words are not crucial for understanding the meaning of the sentence as a whole. However, if the loss of the words in question results in a serious semantic loss to the sentence, then the sentence should somehow be clarified for those who would find the words difficult.

Such clarification can take a number of different forms. If a sentence is unintelligible because it includes a reference to an unfamiliar or difficult concept, then clarification of the sentence requires providing an explanation of that concept; what must be explained is not so much the language as the world that the language is describing. On the other hand, when the concepts are familiar but the language describing them is confusing, the language itself should be changed: an unfamiliar word can be replaced by a more familiar word or phrase, an unfamiliar pronunciation can be clarified by a more familiar one, a sentence can be reorganized so that its words exercise their more usual grammatical functions, or an unfamiliar word can be retained with a diagram or picture added to clarify the meaning.

Most fourth-grade children in Los Angeles read the poem "Casey Jones" in one of their English texts.[3] Before a teacher presents this poem to students who live in a modern urban area like Los Angeles, he should determine what they know about steam-driven

[2] *Language* (New York: Henry Holt and Co., 1933), p. 81.

[3] Paul Roberts, *The Roberts English Series, Book* 4 (New York: Harcourt Brace Jovanovich Inc., 1966), pp. 129, 137.

CASEY JONES

Come all you rounders that want to hear
A story about a brave engineer;
Casey Jones was the hogger's name.
On the Western Pacific he won his fame.

The caller called Casey at half-past four.
He kissed his wife at the station door.
He mounted to the cabin with his orders in his hand,
And took his farewell journey to the promised land.

Put in your water and shovel on your coal,
Stick your head out the window, and watch her roll.
We've got to run her till she leaves the rail,
For we're eight hours late with the Western Mail.

Casey looked at his watch, and his watch was slow.
He looked at the water, and the water was low.
He turned to the fireman, and "Boy," he said,
"We've got to reach Frisco, or we'll all be dead."

Casey pulled up on Reno Hill,
And tooted on the whistle with an awful shrill.
The crossing man knew by the engine's moans
That the man at the throttle was Casey Jones.

Casey pulled up within two miles of the place,
With Number Four staring him right in the face.
He turned to the fireman, said, "Boy you'd better jump,
For there's two locomotives that's going to bump."

Casey said just before he died,
"There's two more roads that I'd like to ride."
The fireman said, "What may they be?"
"Why, the Southern Pacific and the Santa Fe."

locomotives of the sort Casey Jones commanded. Probably few urban fourth-graders have heard of such a train, and far fewer have ridden in one or seen one come by, hissing steam and belching black smoke, the engineer leaning out of the cab window waving regally to children beside the track. For modern urban school children many of the words in this poem refer to objects and situations that do not evoke the elaborate memories shared by their parents and grandparents. Thus, if these students are to fully understand the poem, they must be introduced to an aspect of the American past that has now disappeared: What did Casey Jones's "locomotive" look like? Not like a modern diesel engine. What did the "fireman" do? He didn't put out fires; he fed them. And what is meant by "engineer"? Most of the engineers around Los Angeles today are trained in aerospace or electronics. Why was Casey concerned about the water? What is a "steam engine"? For that matter, what is "coal"? And a "cabin"?—that's what you build in the woods.

Some of the other words in "Casey Jones" may be problematic because they are strange names for familiar things. A "throttle" is identical, in function at least, to an accelerator pedal. "Rounders" are loafers or bums. "Frisco" refers to San Francisco (probably familiar to Los Angeles school children if not to those in Philadelphia or New York). For these words no elaborate diagrams, illustrations, or explanations are necessary. A synonym will do.

One word, *shrill*, may cause confusion because it appears as a noun rather than in its familiar function as an adjective. That difficulty is easily overcome: a *shrill* is a shrill noise. When the poem is read aloud, *Santa Fe* may cause some trouble because it should rhyme with *be*. But if *Santa Fe* is pronounced in a different way, most fourth-graders should recognize it as the name of a city and perhaps also a railroad named after that city.

Recognizing and Simplifying Difficult Sentence Structures

It is obvious that some sentences with familiar vocabulary are nonetheless difficult to understand, and often their difficulty seems to be a matter of structure: the way in which the meanings of words combine to form the meaning of an entire sentence. Just what about the structure of a sentence makes it difficult is far from obvious, however. Some would say that the longer the sentence, the greater its difficulty; but surely this is not an adequate explanation. Many people, in casual conversation, preface all their remarks with the conjunction *and*; as a result, even their longest response is, technically speaking, only one sentence—often one exceedingly long sentence. But such a sentence is no more difficult to understand than a comparable string of sentences with the *ands* left out or replaced by *um* or *ah*. This suggests that sentence length is not always an accurate indication of syntactic difficulty;

certainly not where conjoined English sentences are concerned. But the exception represented by conjoined English sentences can be side stepped if, instead of measuring the length of sentences, we measure the length of minimal independent sentence units (an independent clause together with all clauses or phrases modifying it). Such minimal independent units or minimal terminal units, called *T-units*, are easy to identify. Simply separate each sentence into the smallest possible units that can stand alone as complete sentences. Kellogg W. Hunt uses the following unpunctuated essay written by a fourth-grader to illustrate the concept of T-units.[4]

> I like the movie we saw about Moby Dick the white whale the captain said if you can kill the white whale Moby Dick I will give this gold to the one that can do it and it is worth sixteen dollars they tried and tried but while they were trying they killed a whale and used the oil for the lamps they almost caught the white whale.

Although the number of sentences in this essay can vary depending upon the punctuation, the number of T-units remains unchanged at six:

1. I like the movie we saw about Moby Dick, the white whale.
2. The captain said, if you can kill the white whale, Moby Dick, I will give this gold to the one that can do it.
3. And it is worth sixteen dollars.
4. They tried and tried.
5. But while they were trying, they killed a whale and used the oil for the lamps.
6. They almost caught the white whale.

Even when long sentences contain subordinate as well as coordinate clauses, they are not necessarily difficult. Consider the clause structure in the following nursery rhyme:

> This is the farmer sowing his corn
> That kept the cock that crowed in the morn
> That waked the priest all shaven and shorn
> That married the man all tattered and torn

---

[4] *Grammatical Structures Written at Three Grade Levels*, NCTE Research Report no. 3 (Champaign, Ill.: National Council of Teachers of English, 1965), pp. 20–21.

That kissed the maiden all forlorn
That milked the cow with the crumpled horn
That tossed the dog
That worried the cat
That killed the rat
That ate the malt
That lay in the house
That Jack built.

This entire verse is a single sentence in which every line after the first begins a subordinate (relative) clause modifying the noun phrase that ends the immediately preceding line. And yet this poem is simple enough to appeal to preschool children. What, then, in addition to length can make the structure of a sentence difficult to understand? Here are two suggestions:

(*a*) Sentences may be difficult to understand when their structure is unusual or unfamiliar. Students may be confused by sentence structures that are no longer commonly used (for example, Shakespeare's *What think you?* in place of the modern form *What do you think?*) and by the liberties poets and other writers sometimes take with normal word order. Students in a high-school English class were asked to paraphrase the following sentence from Coleridge's *Rime of the Ancient Mariner:*

Ah wretch! said they, the bird to slay,
That made the breeze to blow.

Here are some of their responses:[5]

— They said, "Ah wretch" to the bird they wanted to slay because he made the breezes blow.

— Don't kill that bird, the wretch said, it broke the air in flight.

— They said I am a wretch for slaying the bird which made the breezes blow.

— As they were going to slay a bird which made the breeze blow, they said "Ah Wretch!"

[5] These examples òf student misunderstanding are cited in Seymour Chatman, "Reading Literature as Problem-Solving," in *Linguistics in the Classroom,* ed. Thomas H. Wetmore (Champaign, Ill.: National Council of Teachers of English, 1963), pp. 32–33.

— Ah wicked one! they said, the breeze started blowing because you killed the poor bird.

— Ah wretch! they said, slay that bird that made the breeze blow.

— It is a shame that it is so windy.

— They said to slay the bird that just flew by.

— Ah wretch they said as the movement of their ax which was to slay the bird escaped him.

(*b*) Sentences may be difficult to understand when they contain clauses that interrupt one another. When a sentence contains two clauses, they may simply be spoken or written one after the other in sequence. A sentence consisting of two conjoined clauses (clauses joined by a conjunction) follows this sequential arrangement:[6]

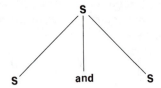

If a sentence of this type were spelled out, it might look like this:

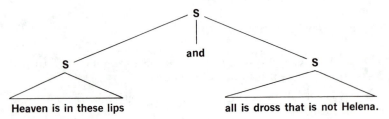

[6] S stands for *sentence*. This use of the word *sentence* is confusing since most traditional grammar books would label the S's on either side of the *and* as clauses rather than sentences. However, the distinction between clauses and sentences breaks down when the structure of language is viewed on a deeper or more abstract level. The sentencelike units which linguists describe at this abstract level can form either independent sentences or clauses (or even phrases or single words) in more complex sentences. Anyone who knows how to speak English knows how to take a sentence containing many clauses and break it down into many sentences of one clause each. In the same way, anyone who knows how to speak English knows how to combine a group of one-clause sentences into a single multiclause sentence.

Even when a sentence contains one or more subordinate clauses, as long as one clause does not interrupt another, comprehension is not taxed. The sentence *As I was going to St. Ives, I met a man with seven wives* might be said to "contain" three smaller sentences:

1. I was going to St. Ives.
2. I met a man.
3. The man had seven wives.

The first of these sentences appears in the larger sentence as a subordinate adverbial clause, the second as the main clause, and the third as an adjectival phrase modifying *a man*. In the total compound sentence, none of these three subsentences interrupts another.

On the other hand, the sentence *People who live in glass houses shouldn't throw stones* contains three component sentences that do interrupt one another:

1. People shouldn't throw stones.
2. People live in houses.
3. Houses are glass.

As the diagram below shows, sentence 2 (S_2) interrupts sentence 1 (S_1), and sentence 3 (S_3) interrupts sentence 2.

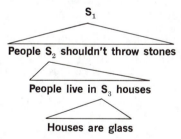

In this particular example, the interruptions are short ones. Sentence 3 has been reduced to a single adjective, *glass*, and the entire interruption of sentence 1 is only five words long.

A more extreme example can be created by rearranging some of the clauses of "The House that Jack Built." In the following, somewhat monstrous sentence the main clause is interrupted by no less than fifty-four words.

The cock that waked the priest all shaven and shorn that married the man all tattered and torn that kissed the maiden all forlorn that milked the cow with the crumpled horn that tossed the dog that worried the cat that killed the rat that ate the malt that lay in the house that Jack built crowed in the morn.

A child's nursery rhyme has become a burden even on the memory span of adults.

The situation could be worse. Consider what happens when we construct a sentence containing one interruption within another interruption within another interruption:

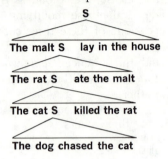

The resulting sentence is literally unintelligible:

The malt that the rat that the cat that the dog chased killed ate lay in the house.

On the basis of these and other similar examples, two corollaries can be added to the original assertion that sentences may be difficult to understand when one clause interrupts another. First, the longer the interruption, the greater the increase in difficulty and, second, interruptions within interruptions may produce total unintelligibility.[7]

The discussion of sentence difficulty so far has considered only cases in which a single sentence occurs in isolation. In cases where the sentence occurs within a longer utterance, another "rule" must be introduced: Difficult sentences make paragraphs and other

---

[7] This second corollary appears not to apply to the sentence *People who live in glass houses shouldn't throw stones,* even though this sentence contains one interruption within another. Perhaps, in order to impair intelligibility both interruptions must be at least two words in length.

larger linguistic units difficult to understand insofar as an understanding of the sentence is prerequisite to an understanding of the larger unit. As with difficult words, there is a fairly simple way to determine the semantic importance of a sentence to a larger linguistic unit: Consider the utterance or passage with the sentence removed. If little meaning is lost or if the intended reader could supply lost meaning from other "context clues," the semantic importance of the sentence is low. To the extent that the removal of the sentence produces irredeemable semantic loss in the total utterance or passage, the semantic importance of the sentence is great and the structure of the sentence should be simplified.[8]

[8] These suggestions for estimating and altering linguistic difficulty represent one writer's synthesis of available research findings. It seems probable that the grammatical features discussed here are useful indicators of sentence intelligibility. But the issue is far from settled. The reader should certainly not conclude that *only* those features mentioned here contribute to sentence intelligibility.

One technique for measuring sentence intelligibility or "readability" that has been omitted here is the Cloze procedure. In this procedure, every fifth word is omitted from a passage, and a reader is then asked to supply these missing words. The percentage of the total that the reader is able to guess indicates the difficulty of the passage for that reader. A score of 57 percent indicates that the passage is easy enough to be assigned for independent study. For a further discussion of the Cloze procedure see John R. Bormuth, "The Cloze Readability Procedure," *Elementary English* 45 (April 1968): 429–36. For use as a part of the diagnostic and remedial techniques discussed here the Cloze procedure has one serious disadvantage: the procedure indicates the level of intelligibility, but it fails to indicate *why* the passage in question is at that level. It does not separate cognitive from linguistic difficulties; nor does it isolate different forms of linguistic difficulty. Consequently it provides no indication of why a particular passage is difficult for a particular student, nor any basis for determining how the passage might be altered to make it less difficult.

Another technique for estimating sentence intelligibility that has been intentionally omitted from the discussion in this text is based on the assumption that the greater the number of transformation rules involved in converting the conceptual or deep structure of a sentence into the surface structure, the more difficult that sentence will be to understand. This assumption is doubtful, and in any case a measurement of intelligibility based on transformational complexity would become embroiled in current debates over the structure of transformational rules. Indeed, this view of transformational complexity related to sentence intelligibility is, at some points, in conflict with the view presented in this text. The transformational-complexity hypothesis would predict that the additional deletion transformations necessary to generate an adjective from an underlying relative clause should reduce the intelligibility of a sentence. Thus the sentence *The boy who is unpleasant disrupted the class* should be easier to understand than *The unpleasant boy disrupted the class*. However, the claim here is that the latter sentence should be easier to understand since the interruption of the main clause is shorter (one word rather than three).

The procedure for simplifying a structurally difficult sentence will depend upon the nature of the structural difficulty. If the sentence is difficult because its structure is unusual or unfamiliar, changes in word order and function words[9] will generally make the structure more familiar:

Into the valley of death rode the six hundred.	The six hundred rode into the valley of death.
Ah wretch! said they, the bird to slay, that made the breeze to blow.	"You're a wretch," they said, "because you slew the bird that made the breeze blow."

If a sentence is difficult to understand because one clause interrupts another, the sentence can be simplified either by making each clause a separate sentence—

The malt that the rat that the cat that the dog chased killed ate lay in the house.	The malt lay in the house. The rat ate that malt. The cat killed that rat. The dog chased that cat.

—or by rearranging the structure of the sentence so that the clauses no longer interrupt one another:

The malt that the rat that the cat that the dog chased killed ate lay in the house.	In the house lay the malt that was eaten by the rat that was killed by the cat that was chased by the dog.

Consider the case of a high-school history teacher who must choose among three possible texts for her ninth-grade American history class. She knows that many of the students in her class are not native speakers of English and that they may therefore have trouble if the language used in the text is too difficult. In choosing among the texts, she wants to consider the syntactic difficulty of each (in addition to the difficulty of vocabulary, appropriateness and clarity of illustrations, organization and choice of subjects covered, and so on). To compare syntactic difficulty, she compares

[9] Function words are words whose *primary* purpose in a sentence is to relate the meaning of other words rather than to add new meaning. In the sentence *There is nothing more for me to say,* the words *there, for,* and *to* are clearly function words since by themselves they have little or no meaning.

the three passages, one from each text, which appear below starting on the following page.

First she determines the number of words per sentence on the assumption that, in general, shorter sentences are easier to read than longer ones. By dividing the total number of words in each passage by the number of sentences in that same passage she arrives at the following comparison:

Average number of words per sentence

Passage A	24.6
Passage B	20.0
Passage C	16.9

But these differences in sentence length might reflect a difference in the authors' tendencies to conjoin separable sentence-length units (so-called T-units) to form long but easily comprehended sentences. So the teacher searches the three passages for sentences containing two or more T-units. For example, in passage A the T-unit *American tea dealers, of course, protested against the unfair competition from a giant corporation* and the T-unit *but tea drinkers also resented the new law, for they considered it an attempt to trick them into accepting taxation by Parliament*[10] join to form a single sentence. And passage B contains two sentences that are two T-units long: *Foreign competition had captured many of its markets, and the company soon had 17,000,000 pounds of surplus tea stored in British warehouses;* and *British lawmakers had expected American merchants and storekeepers to resent the fact that the East India Company could bypass them in selling directly to customers, but they had not counted on general colonial hostility.* Based on these findings, the teacher divides the total number of words in each passage by the total number of T-units to arrive at a more accurate measurement of relative sentence complexity:

Average number of words per T-unit

Passage A	22.5
Passage B	17.9
Passage C	15.4

[10] A case could be made for considering this two T-units rather than one T-unit.

According to this tabulation, passage C is syntactically the simplest of the three. But the difference in difficulty between C and B is not as great as that between B and A.

As a final comparison of syntactic complexity among the three passages, the teacher looks for instances where one phrase or clause interrupts another. (For example, in the sentence *The colonists, who had a reputation as inveterate tea drinkers, were expected to swallow the Townshend tax along with the cheap tea*, the clause *who had a reputation as inveterate tea drinkers* interrupts the main clause *The colonists . . . were expected to swallow the Townshend tax along with the cheap tea*. Passage A contains five such interrupting clauses (an average of 0.42 per T-unit); passage B contains two (an average of 0.10 per T-unit); and passage C contains two (an average of 0.18 per T-unit). Moreover, the interruptions in passage A contain 8.4 words each; those in passage B average 7.5 words each; and those in passage C average 4.0 words each. These figures support the earlier evidence that passage A, with both the most and the longest interrupting clauses, is syntactically the most difficult.

PASSAGE A: The Tea Act revived the quarrel[11]

By 1773, the East India Company, a great corporation which largely monopolized both the commerce and the government of the British possessions in India, found itself in serious financial difficulties. The Tea Act was passed to help the company.

This law authorized the company to sell tea directly to retailers in North America, without paying any taxes except the tea tax left over from the Townshend duties. In the past, the company had been required to pay various taxes in Great Britain and had been allowed to sell its tea only to British merchants, who in turn sold it to American merchants, who then distributed it among retailers in the colonies. Under the new law, with the middlemen's profits and most of the taxes eliminated, the company would be able to undersell all competitors. The colonists, who had a reputation as inveterate tea drinkers, were expected to swallow the Townshend tax along

[11] These three passages are from the following sources: Passage A—Richard N. Current, Alexander DeConde, and Harris L. Dante, *United States History* (Glenview, Ill.: Scott, Foresman and Co., 1967), pp. 50–51. Copyright © 1967 by Scott, Foresman and Company. Reprinted by permission of the publisher. Passage B—Jack Allen and John L. Betts, *History: USA* (New York: American Book Co., 1967), pp. 66–67. Passage C—Margaret G. Mackey, *Your Country's History* (Boston: Ginn and Co., 1966), p. 121.

with the cheap tea and, in doing so, to provide large profits for the East India Company.

The reaction in North America surprised the British authorities. American tea dealers, of course, protested against the unfair competition from a giant corporation, but tea drinkers also resented the new law, for they considered it an attempt to trick them into accepting taxation by Parliament. The colonists took oaths to use none of the company's tea. When its tea ships arrived in colonial ports, angry crowds compelled them either to turn back or to leave their cargo, unsold, in warehouses. In Boston harbor, the followers of Samuel Adams, disguised as Indians, boarded the ships and threw the tea into the harbor.

PASSAGE B: The Tea Act of 1773 Creates a New Crisis

In May, 1773, a course of events began that finally led to open rebellion. The giant British East India Company, a trading corporation whose stockholders included many members of Parliament, had fallen upon hard times. Foreign competition had captured many of its markets, and the company soon had 17,000,000 pounds of surplus tea stored in British warehouses. To aid the company, Lord North induced Parliament to enact the legislation known as the Tea Act of 1773. By this act, the East India Company was given a monopoly of the sale of tea in the colonies, and was exempted from paying any British taxes. This meant that the company would be able to sell its tea to Americans at a price cheaper than smuggled tea. Englishmen in England had to pay considerably more.

Lord North and Parliament sadly misjudged the colonials' reaction to this Tea Act. British lawmakers had expected American merchants and storekeepers to resent the fact that the East India Company could bypass them in selling directly to customers, but they had not counted on general colonial hostility. As it turned out, Americans condemned the legislation as a trick to get them to accept the tea tax by reducing the price of tea to a new low. What would be the next step, they asked. What other bankrupt British companies would be saved by dumping their products on the colonials?

Once more the radicals swung into action to resist the new British law with a renewed boycott of all British goods. They were especially determined that East India Company tea would never be sold in America. In New York and Philadelphia, bands of men—merchants and storekeepers among them—met the tea ships and persuaded the captains to return without unloading the despised cargo. In Charleston, the tea was unloaded but stored in warehouses. But it was in Boston, under the genius of Sam Adams, that the most dramatic event took place. On a December night in 1773, a group of about 50 citizens dressed as Mohawk Indians slipped aboard the tea ships in Boston Harbor and purposefully tossed 342 chests of tea into the murky harbor.

PASSAGE C: The tea tax led to a Tea Party

In 1773, the British East India Company, which was losing money, asked the government for help. Parliament obliged the company by giving it the right to sell tea directly to the colonies without having to pay a tax on the tea in Britain. However, the company was to collect a tea tax from the colonies.

When the colonists heard this they knew that the East India Company would enforce the tea tax and there could be no more tea smuggling. Many colonial merchants would be put out of business. And, if the colonists did buy from the company, they would be required to pay a tax and thus admit the right of Britain to tax them.

In December of that year the first ship of the East India Company sailed into Boston harbor. It received an unusual welcome. Boston patriots, dressed as Indians, went aboard the ships at night, broke open the tea chests and threw the tea into the bay. No tax would be paid on that tea!

Controlling Response Complexity[12]

Any speaker of a language can understand more of its words and sentence structures than he can produce; the passive skill of understanding language develops ahead of the active skill of producing language. Children two years old can say only a few words and "sentences," but they understand a good deal of what adults say to them. Most educated English-speaking adults can understand Shakespeare's language at least reasonably well, but few if any can produce it accurately. Many people who can read or listen with understanding to a foreign language cannot speak or write that language. But it is unthinkable that anyone could speak and write a language without a passive understanding of its written and spoken forms. So it is that some students can understand the lan-

---

[12] This section draws many ideas from Earl W. Stevick, *A Workbook in Language Teaching* (New York: Abingdon Press, 1963), pp. 59–68.

guage or dialect used in the classroom but cannot produce that language or dialect fluently.

To teach such students effectively, a teacher must find ways to test how well they understand the subject matter without at the same time testing their ability to produce standard English. Whenever a student is asked to demonstrate his knowledge or understanding through speaking, these two variables are compounded. Teachers must realize that their questions and other requests for a verbal response can be difficult linguistically or conceptually or in both ways. Linguistic difficulty may be difficulty in understanding the teacher's question or request—the sort of difficulty discussed in the first part of this chapter; or it may also be difficulty in producing the language necessary for a response.

Listed below in order of increasing linguistic difficulty are four types of response, each followed by examples of requests for that kind of response:

1. *"Yes" or "No" response*

   a. Did Brutus kill Caesar?
   b. Did Mark Antony admire Caesar?
   c. Does the assertion, "God is omnipotent," imply a contradiction?

2. *Response requiring repetition of word or phrase*

   a. Did you write the assignment with a pencil or with a pen?
   b. Which turns red litmus paper blue—acids or alkalis?
   c. In learning to read, a child should learn:
      —which sounds are represented by each letter of the alphabet.
      —which letters of the alphabet represent each sound.
      —both of the above.

3. *Response requiring a word or phrase not supplied in the question*

   a. What color is the litmus paper?
   b. What letter comes between *d* and *f?*
   c. What is the difference in sound-wave frequency between any two tones an octave apart?

4. Response requiring extensive original language

    a. What did you do last Saturday?
    b. Why didn't the litmus paper turn blue when we dipped it in the vinegar?
    c. What made Brutus want to kill Caesar?

The questions within each of the four response categories represent a range of cognitive difficulty:[13] the *a* questions are intellectually less demanding than the *b*'s, which are in turn less demanding than the *c*'s. Question 4*a*, for example, requires the linguistic ability to produce an extensive original utterance which is grammatically correct and semantically appropriate. But this same question requires no cognitive sophistication beyond a knowledge of a few of the speaker's own recent experiences. Question 2*c*, on the other hand, requires linguistically only the ability to repeat or copy a phrase, but conceptually it requires the cognitive capacity to distinguish two closely related skills and to evaluate the appropriateness of each to a complex learning task.

A teacher aware of both the cognitive and the linguistic difficulty of the questions he asks can vary each independently. The following examples suggest different ways in which a teacher might use this skill.

1. Suppose a student consistently omits answering comprehension questions covering reading assignments. In many, probably most, instances the teacher's response would be limited to one or more of the following:

    a. He gives the student a low grade.
    b. He tells the student what the answer should have been.
    c. He tells the student to reread the assigned passage.

The low grade makes official the fact that the appropriate response was not given; but will a low grade increase the probability of future learning? The threat of low grades may prod some students to learning, but that sort of prodding may not be what this particular student needs. Giving the student the correct answers may

---

[13] The notion of "cognitive difficulty" cannot be developed in detail here. For further clarification of this notion see Benjamin S. Bloom, ed., *Taxonomy of Educational Objectives, Handbook I: Cognitive Domain* (New York: David McKay Co., Inc., 1956).

have some value if the objective of the lesson is only that the student come to know the answers to the questions he has been asked. But then, why not simply give the student the answers in the first place rather than forcing him to weed them out of a reading assignment? More than likely, however, the reading comprehension questions were simply a means of sampling the total knowledge the student was to have gained from the assigned reading. In that case, giving him the correct answers does not meet the real learning objectives. Rereading the assigned passages might help some students, but perhaps this student does not know how to read.

In the situation just described, a teacher responded to a failure to answer reading comprehension questions without first determining the causes of that failure. Was the student bored? hostile? tired? ignorant? Different causes demand different responses from the teacher. When, as in this case, a student's demonstration of his learning involves the use of language, the teacher must weigh the possibility that the student lacks the language skills necessary for an appropriate response. Perhaps the student understands the questions but lacks the linguistic skills necessary for answers. To determine whether or not this is an actual cause of the student's failure, the teacher might begin by determining the linguistic difficulty of the questions the student failed to answer. For the sake of this example, suppose that each of the questions required a response in extensive original language (see level 4, above). Would the student be able to supply the information requested if the linguistic demands were less severe? To find out, the teacher can reduce the linguistic difficulty and reask the question. Instead of

> In your own words, explain why the Pilgrims traveled to the east coast of North America and settled in Plymouth. (level 4)

the teacher might ask:

> What did the Pilgrims hope to find in America? (level 3)

or

> Why did the Pilgrims come to America: to farm the rich soil? to trade furs with the Indians? to worship as they pleased? or to escape the crowded conditions in Europe? (level 2)

or

> Did the Pilgrims come to America to trade furs with the
> Indians? (level 1)

2. A student fails a thirty-five-question midterm examination by answering only twelve of the thirty-five questions correctly. The teacher wonders whether the difficulty is cognitive or linguistic. To find out, she analyzes the student's responses in the following way:

		CORRECT RESPONSES AT VARIOUS LEVELS OF LINGUISTIC AND COGNITIVE DIFFICULTY				
		Level of Linguistic Difficulty				
		1 (lowest)	2	3	4	Total
Level of Cognitive Difficulty	*a* (lowest)	2/3	2/2	2/4	0/9	6/18
	b	2/2	0/0	3/10	0/1	5/13
	c	0/0	1/1	0/0	0/3	1/4
	Total:	4/5	3/3	5/14	0/13	12/35

NOTE: The fractions in each box should be read:
Number of questions answered correctly/Total number of questions asked

Of the thirty-five questions asked, three were both cognitively and linguistically on the lowest level of difficulty, and of those three the student answered two correctly. Nine of the thirty-five questions had lowest cognitive difficulty and highest linguistic difficulty; the student answered none of these questions correctly. His total score was 12/35 or 34 percent, but he scored 7/8 or 88 percent on level-1 and level-2 questions, which, although linguistically easy, represent all three levels of cognitive difficulty. On the other hand, the student correctly answered none of the thirteen linguistically most difficult questions (level 4), even though nine of the thirteen were on the lowest level of cognitive difficulty. The teacher, after looking at this chart, might suspect that his student knew the answers to more than 34 percent of the questions but was unable to express these answers in written English.

3. Young children are frequently too shy to speak in a classroom situation. In order to establish communication, the teacher might ask a series of questions on a familiar subject, gradually increasing the linguistic complexity of the response requested:

TEACHER: Do you know what day it is tomorrow? (level 1)
CHILD: (*nods*)
TEACHER: What day is that? (level 3)
CHILD: (*no response—teacher returns to lower level*)
TEACHER: Is it Christmas? (level 1)
CHILD: (*laughs*) No.
TEACHER: Is it Thanksgiving? (level 1)
CHILD: Yes.
TEACHER: Are you going to eat a lot? (level 1)
CHILD: Yes.
TEACHER: Are you going to eat turkey or cheeseburgers? (level 2)
CHILD: (*smiles*) Turkey.
TEACHER: What else will you eat besides turkey? (level 3)
CHILD: Potatoes and milk—and you know what? I got a cat and he likes milk, and he likes spaghetti too.

. . .

Lest teachers of English with limited time or limited understanding of linguistic theory become discouraged, here are two parting words of encouragement. This chapter has a central theme that can guide even the most harried teacher: verbal fluency and dexterity are not the same as intellectual prowess. The capacity to express an idea in complex English is not the same as the capacity to understand that idea. And finally, English teachers who are native speakers of English need not rely entirely on formal linguistic estimates of language complexity; based on their own intuitions they can rephrase sentences, substituting simpler syntactic constructions and simpler vocabulary. This intuitive, largely unconscious capacity to rephrase for simplicity is part of an adult's ability as a language user. Teachers as well as their students are natural language learners.

TEACHING ABOUT LANGUAGE

That teachers who know about the nature of language are best able to help their students master language-related skills in school has been one of the central arguments of this book. But, the argument continues, although English teachers need to know something about the nature of English, they *need* not pass this knowledge on to their students. The sense of urgency many teachers feel to teach grammar is unwarranted. Students can grow into educated, literate adults without studying English linguistics.

So might the case rest, albeit uneasily. However, though studying English linguistics cannot create writers or spellers of English, it can be fascinating, and useful, not only for English teachers but for students in English classes as well—if they know how (and how not) to use it. This last chapter is intended not as a definitive statement to English teachers who may wish to teach English linguistics to their students, but as a bit of initial counsel to nudge them in the right direction.

Linguistics for Students of Composition and Literature

English teachers are not the only ones who teach English linguistics. It is taught in anthropology and sociology classes because language differences often provide clues to differences in cultures or social structures; it is taught in psychology classes because human behavior more often than not involves linguistic behavior; and because philosophical arguments often lead to a consideration of the language through which such arguments are expressed, linguistics is discussed in philosophy classes as well. The list of subject areas to which linguistics applies can be extended further to such disciplines as mathematics, medicine, history, communications, computer science, and acoustics. But, since this is a book primarily for English teachers, the discussion here will be limited to the value a knowledge of English linguistics can have for students in English classes, where the primary concern is composition or literature.

Composition. The most popular reason for teaching English linguistics in elementary and secondary schools is that it supposedly helps students write better. The worse the writer, the more he needs to know about English grammar—or so the traditional argument runs. But that argument is supported neither by the experience of most teachers nor by the understanding linguists have gained about how language is learned and how the mind and vocal organs function in the production and perception of language. As explained in earlier chapters, knowing *how* to use a language does not require and is not demonstrably facilitated by knowing *about* that language.

The chairman of the English department at a highly regarded high school in the Los Angeles area no longer insists that the teachers on his staff teach *about* English grammar. He explains that neither the teachers nor their students saw any sense in it, and that the high degree of success achieved by his former students in university-level English courses did not diminish when grammar was dropped from the high school's curriculum. Many other English teachers have made similar observations, but are less willing to admit it.

Such reluctance is unnecessary. An impressive body of educational research conducted over the past half-century has been directed at one or another aspect of the relationship between knowing grammar and the mastery of composition skills. The state of this research from the beginning of this century up through the early 1960s has been summarized by Henry C. Meckel, as a part of his review of research on teaching composition. After considering the results of studies measuring the effect of a knowledge of grammar on a variety of composition skills—including the ability to punctuate and the ability to recognize faults in sentence structure—Meckel begins his summary with the following remark: "There is no research evidence that grammar as traditionally taught has any appreciable effect on the improvement of writing skill."[1]

The emergence of transformational-generative grammar during the past decade again raised the question: Will teaching this new kind of grammar aid in improving composition skills? Apparently not. Although recent research projects do report occasional changes in the writing of students who have received special formal training in transformational grammar,[2] such changes are sometimes negative (students write less) and sometimes difficult to interpret (students use more subordination). Mark Lester, a linguist and teacher of composition, after considering the value of transformational grammar in teaching composition, concludes unequivocally: "There simply appears to be no correlation between a writer's conscious study of grammar and his ability to write."[3]

Learning about grammar (studying or memorizing grammatical rules) is different from doing grammatical drills (practicing the controlled manipulation of sentence structure), even though such

---

[1] "Research on Teaching Composition and Literature," in *Handbook of Research in Teaching*, ed. Nathaniel L. Gage (Chicago: Rand McNally, 1963), p. 981.

[2] Two such research projects are reported in Donald Bateman and Frank Zidonis, *The Effect of a Study of Transformational Grammar on the Writing of Ninth and Tenth Graders*, NCTE Research Report no. 6 (Champaign, Ill.: National Council of Teachers of English, 1966); and Nathan S. Blount, Wayne C. Frederick, and Shelby L. Johnson, *The Effect of a Study of Grammar on the Writing of Eighth Grade Students*, Wisconsin Research and Development Center for Cognitive Learning Technical Report no. 69 (Madison: University of Wisconsin, December 1968).

[3] "The Value of Transformational Grammar in Teaching Composition," in *Readings in Applied Transformational Grammar*, ed. Mark Lester (New York: Holt, Rinehart and Winston, Inc., 1970), p. 204.

drills are frequently organized around some grammatical rule. The student who is told that the -s inflection on verbs signals a present tense indicative form with a third-person singular subject is learning one fact about the grammar of standard English; the student who is asked to write or copy a set of sentences contrasting this -s ending with other verbal inflections is producing or repeating language in a controlled way. This latter student may but need not be told the rule of grammar governing the exercise he is performing. Exercises involving the controlled manipulation of language structure have been used with some success in teaching comprehension of foreign languages; such exercises may also be helpful in teaching composition skills.

In a recent study, John C. Mellon discovered that junior-high-school students could be trained in sentence combining so that the sentences they wrote were significantly longer and more complex than those produced by children of the same age who had not received such training.[4] The subjects of the study became skilled at combining two or more simple sentences according to a regular pattern (defined by a transformational rule) to form a more complex sentence. For example, given the following sentences—

A volume of poetry lay unguarded near the library exit.
The volume was thin.
The volume was brown.
The volume was leather-bound.
The volume was a rare first edition.
The volume was compiled by Dr. Johnson.

—one of the students might respond with the following:

A thin brown leather-bound volume of poetry, a rare first edition, compiled by Dr. Johnson lay unguarded near the table.

The favorable influence of Mellon's technique may encourage many English teachers to provide their classes with similar sen-

[4] *Transformational Sentence-Combining*, NCTE Research Report no. 10 (Champaign, Ill.: National Council of Teachers of English, 1969). Mellon's research and its implications for English teachers is discussed in Charles R. Cooper, "A No-Grammar Approach to Sentence Power: John C. Mellon's Sentence-Combining Games," *California English Journal* 7, No. 1 (February 1971): 35–40.

tence-combining exercises; however, enthusiasm for sentence-combining training should be tempered by a practical analysis of its results. The more complex sentences that sentence-combining drills encouraged Mellon's subjects to produce are no different from the sorts of sentences those same children would have begun to produce at a later age as a result of the natural maturation of their language skills. At best, these drills simply speed up a natural process: they encourage children to produce grammatically more complex sentences sooner. Moreover, the length or complexity of a sentence is no measure of its appropriateness or literary value. A good writer not only knows how to reexpress his ideas by combining, separating, or restructuring sentences, he also understands the effect each process will have upon his writing and consequently is able to choose the process that will give him the desired expression of his ideas.

Teaching about grammar seems to hold little promise as an aid to teaching composition at an elementary or intermediate level. However, the verdict on introducing formal study of English grammar into advanced composition classes is not quite so clear-cut. The value a knowledge of English linguistics has for the writer compares with the value a knowledge of color physics and the psychology of color perception has for the painter. A painter can perceive color and employ this perception in the creation of visual art without understanding whatever explanation of his perception a physicist or psychologist could give. And yet some artists have been intrigued by formal studies of the properties of light and color and by scientific explanations of the human perception of those properties. The artist who finds the vocabulary of the physicist or the psychologist useful in talking to himself or to others about what he is doing is probably already an advanced amateur or practicing professional, however. No one would dream of teaching a beginner (especially a young beginner) how to paint by requiring an introductory course in the physics of color and the psychology of color perception; usually he is given a brush and allowed to explore and develop his own capacity to perceive and arrange colors.

Similarly, the beginning writer should be allowed to develop his capacity to express himself in writing without first being subjected to lessons in grammar. The composition teacher is the student writer's first audience; he should be receptive, anxious to understand and to appreciate, and offer criticism only to the extent that the student is able to receive and use it without becoming antagonized or discouraged. When a student writes *Because the murder weapon was found in his room, the policeman arrested the chauffeur,* his teacher can explain the confusion over modification without using technical vocabulary: "Some readers might think that the weapon is in the policeman's room because the words *his room* are closer to *policeman* than to *chauffeur.* You can write the same idea in a way that creates no confusion about whose room the weapon is in. Just move *Because the murder weapon was found in his room* to the end of the sentence after *chauffeur.*" This remedial discussion of style in writing employs no grammatical terms beyond *word* and *sentence.*

To be sure, these same comments could have been expressed using more grammatical terms: "In this sentence the pronoun *his* is closer to the noun *policeman* than to the intended referent noun *chauffeur.* This confusion as to the referent can be avoided by rearranging the word order so that the adverbial clause follows the main clause." What is gained by the use of grammatical terminology in this second version of the explanation? As long as the discussion is limited to that one sentence, probably nothing—the jargon in the second explanation will baffle more beginning writers than it enlightens.

With more advanced students of composition, however, a teacher may wish to discuss not a single sentence but all sentences sharing a grammatical pattern. Confronting the referent problem mentioned above, he would find it virtually impossible to talk about a class of sentences without using the vocabulary necessary to define that class: "Sentence adverbials in English, whether they are words, phrases, or whole clauses, can occur in at least three positions in a sentence—at the beginning, between the subject and predicate, and at the end. Pronouns occurring in such adverbial phrases or clauses can either precede or follow their referent in the main clause. Because of this flexibility in the position of sentence adverbials and in the relative position of pronouns within adverbials and their noun referents, grammatical sentences can be produced in which the pronoun is separated from its referent by one or more other nouns. Such sentences, although grammatical, frequently create difficulties in interpretation since the natural tendency is to associate a pronoun with the closest noun of the appropriate number and gender. This confusion can be eliminated by moving the sentence adverbial to a position in the sentence close to the noun referent."

Although such formal generalizations about English syntax may prove useful for experienced writers—the writer capable of generalizing about his language in this way can devise some systematic procedures for recognizing and correcting sentences with grammatical structures prone to misinterpretation—they do no more than describe knowledge that every user of English unconsciously holds. A writer does not need to know *about* such knowledge since he already knows *how* to use it. It is true, however, that stylistic corrections made purely on the basis of unconscious grammatical knowledge may be somewhat haphazard; but this imprecision seems preferable to the problems that arise when a young, inexperienced writer thinks that he must learn about grammar as a prerequisite to writing in his language and therefore becomes discouraged and gives up before he begins.

The advent of the approach to language description known as *generative grammar* has brought with it another application of linguistics that appeals to writers. Generative descriptions of English provide rules whereby a single abstract characterization of sentence meaning can be related to a number of structurally and lexically different sentences all of which express that same meaning. In terms more familiar to writers, the rules define a set of sentences that are stylistically different expressions of the same idea. Such rules provide a partial characterization of what writers mean by *style* and *stylistic variation*. Writers are constantly asking themselves: How can I say this same thing in a slightly different way? The rules of generative grammar can provide a formal, elaborate answer to that question. But again, these rules simply state formally what any writer or teacher of English already knows unconsciously. Knowing such formal rules is obviously not a prerequisite for recognizing and employing stylistic variants.

Writers and composition teachers sometimes expect more from formal grammatical rules than such rules can provide. The junior-high-school teacher who encourages his students to learn the rules of grammar as a way of recognizing and avoiding ungrammatical sentences is expecting too much both of the students and of the rules. As these descriptions account for more and more of the facts of grammatical structure they become more and more complex, defying the comprehension of linguists—let alone that of seventh-grade composition students. And even with such complexity, the rules of grammar formulated so far fail to account for many of the sentences seventh-graders can and do produce.

Writers who look to linguistics as an arbiter of the relative value of stylistic variants also expect too much. As mentioned above, linguistics can provide formal definitions of stylistic variants, but the writer himself must decide which one of the variants available to him is most appropriate for his particular audience, message, and situation.

Literature. Nearly every twentieth-century American who reads Chaucer or Shakespeare finds many passages difficult to understand not only because the words are unfamiliar but because the sentence structures follow rules that do not apply in modern English. Such difficulties cannot be overcome by looking up words in a dictionary, even if the dictionary includes historical meanings. The ultimate authority in the interpretation of sentence structures in Old, Middle, or Early Modern English is a grammar of that form of English. When the interpretation of sentence structure *must* be right (when a scholar is annotating or editing an historical document, or when a critic of early literature writes comments that hinge on sentence meaning), then the authority of a formal historical grammar must be consulted. Linguistics is useful, in some cases indispensable, for the professional and advanced student of English literature.

But what of the beginning reader of Chaucer or Shakespeare? For him, formally stated rules of historical grammar are unnecessary. The capacity shared by all speakers of English to gain passive mastery of foreign dialects applies to dialects separate in time as well as those separate in space. Any English-speaking reader of Chaucer or Shakespeare gradually finds himself coming quite unconsciously to understand most of the grammatical constructions that at first puzzled him. An experienced reader of Shakespeare's English understands sentences like *Would I were a king* to mean the same thing as *I wish I were a king* probably without even realizing that he is understanding a variety of English that no one speaks today. Teachers of historical literature sometimes fail to realize how much they themselves have mastered these earlier forms of English grammar and consequently fail to appreciate the extent of the difficulty their students encounter when they first read or hear them.

Scholars interested in establishing the date at which some passage was composed frequently consider as evidence the grammar or vocabulary used in the passage. Because the rules of English grammar have been constantly changing throughout the history of the language, establishing the grammatical rules followed in a passage can set limits on its date of origin. In a somewhat more complex way, the same principle can be used to differentiate the written works of contemporaneous speakers of the same dialect, for no two people have exactly the same grammatical system. Although the distinguishing characteristics of a given idiolect or personal language system are often hard to measure, they do form a kind of "language print" which can be used in identifying the writings of its owner. When further research has been done in this area, it may be possible to use linguistic evidence to determine, for example, whether Chaucer wrote any or all of the disputed works that some have attributed to him.

The applications of linguistics to literature that have been discussed so far are appropriate mainly for the editor or literary historian; however, linguistics can also be valuable for the literary critic. Since literary critics view the works of other writers in much the same way that any writer must consider and evaluate his own writing, the comments made earlier in this chapter concerning the value of linguistics for writers are also applicable to their critics. Unlike the writer, however, a literary critic must have a technical vocabulary for talking about the style of authors. If concerned with poetry or the poetic quality of prose, for example, literary critics must have a vocabulary for describing the various sound effects that poets employ. Without this specialized vocabulary, their descriptions of style cannot go beyond impressionistic or metaphoric labeling (masculine, pure, natural, oblique, limber, thin, staccato, flowing, involuted).

Meter in English poetry is generally represented as a systematic alternation of stressed and unstressed syllables. But the natural rhythms and stresses of English speech contrast several degrees of stress expressed in several different ways: either by changes in loudness, pitch, tempo, or the quality of vowels. Poetry is the superimposition of a stress-unstress metric system onto the complex natural stress system of English. The artistry of poetry depends in part on the poet's capacity to perform this superimposition, and the critic must in turn be prepared to analyze and discuss the poet's success.

Creative writing constantly takes liberties with the rules normally governing English grammar. A novelist or poet may use sentence structures that are, from the point of view of normal English grammar, ungrammatical. But *ungrammatical* certainly does not mean *bad* or *wrong*. The writer distorts language for artistic ends in the same way the painter distorts visual images. E. E. Cummings, for example, is notorious for his distortion and manipulation of normal syntax. Critics or scholars interested in defining or describing such writing may find it useful to do so in precise terms, and the description of the boundaries of normal syntax that linguistics provides can aid them in their task. Linguistics, however, does not provide a touchstone for critical evaluation of literature. No linguistic description can isolate those properties that distinguish good writing from bad; beauty, depth of feeling, artistic appropriateness cannot be measured linguistically. There is no linguistic formula for discovering great writing.

The Intrinsic Value of Language Study

The study of language need not be justified by its effect on learning academic skills. If man needs or desires to understand himself and other human beings and if education helps satisfy this need, then the study of language does not have to be an aid to reading or writing, or to anything else. Our ability to think, act, feel, and interact as human beings is bound up with our ability to speak to and understand each other. In learning about language, a student is learning about himself: no further justification is necessary. Such learning can start for a child even before he enters school and can continue as long as his capacity to understand and desire to know.

If the school student learns about language in order to learn about himself, then he must learn about his own language—his own dialect and developing idiolect. Almost all the language study in American schools teaches children about a dialect, style, or language other than their own. When a student studies his own language, he learns how to talk about knowledge that he already possesses unconsciously. With a teacher's judicious encouragement, the process can be one of self-discovery in which the student realizes that amazingly intricate and complex system governing the language he uses every day. The goal is self-awareness.

A teacher with this goal in mind for her students might design methods by which to encourage their awareness of language. The following language-awareness games are presented to suggest the possible range of such methods and also to suggest the way in which they can be designed to suit the age and maturity of the learner.

The principle common to all language-awareness games is that everyone wins—everyone gets the right answer. The student-player finds himself able to give one correct answer after the other. The teacher then encourages him to ask himself: How is it that I got the answers so consistently and so easily? Who taught me what the answers are? I must know something that enables me to answer as I do.

Perhaps the easiest of all language games—it can be played with three- and four-year-old children—is the game of opposites. For instance, the teacher says to the child: "Sometimes the bird flies very high; sometimes he flies very . . ." The child supplies the word *low*. Or the teacher might say, "Sometimes the noise of the cars is very soft, but sometimes it is very . . ." And the child supplies the word *loud*. Children can play this game long before they can answer questions like "What is the opposite of *soft*? . . . of *high*?" Once children catch on to the game they consistently give right answers, and when properly praised for their success they play the game enthusiastically. This suggests that even young children organize their vocabularies according to some abstract notion of oppositeness. Although a three-year-old child is several years too young to understand or talk about this concept in an abstract way, he can begin to perceive its operation in his own speech.

Another language game grew from the need to help English teachers understand the difference between the sorts of unconscious grammatical rules that linguists describe and the much more limited rules of "grammar" that are traditionally taught in school. Many teachers believe that unless a speaker is taught grammar in school, his language is lawless; the following language-awareness game is useful in dispelling this misconception. The object of the game is to place all of the following adjectives—*lovely, the, maple, all, many, green*—in front of the noun *trees* in an order such that they form a noun phrase with all of the adjectives modifying the noun *trees*. Within a few minutes almost every player comes up with the right answer:

> *all the many lovely green maple trees.*

Perhaps someone suggests

> *all the many lovely maple green trees*

or

> *the many lovely all green maple trees.*

But someone else usually points out that in those phrases *maple* and *all* modify *green,* and consequently the rule of the game (all adjectives modify *trees*) has not been followed. The teacher-player comes to see that this set of six adjectives can only occur in one order and that speakers of English immediately recognize that right order. Since the number of conceivable orders the six adjectives might assume is 720, this question is raised: How is it that almost all the players arrive at that same one correct ordering? Were they taught some adjective-ordering rule in school? No. And yet there must be some rule that leads all but a few players to the one correct ordering.

Both of the games described so far only begin the process whereby a speaker of English perceives himself to be following rules. Some of the more elaborate language-awareness games can lead the learner to at least a partial awareness of what these rules are like by encouraging him to make statements *about* his language capacity. A convenient subject for such a game might be the pronunciation of the regular past tense marker, which in English is spelled *-ed* at the end of a verb and pronounced in one of three different ways depending on the final sound of that verb. A past-tense-marker pronunciation game might follow this plan:

1. The students determine how many different pronunciations they know for the spelling -ed as a marker of the past tense. The three pronunciations (which a class of students will predictably arrive at) can be represented on the board:

[-t]   [-d]   [-əd]

2. The teacher gives a set of English verbs in their unmarked, infinitive form. The class will with predictable unanimity associate the one appropriate past tense pronunciation with each verb. The verbs can then be written on the board under the appropriate pronunciation:

[-t]	[-d]	[-əd]
hoped	played	waited
dropped	died	confronted
packed	tatooed	condescended
laughed	grabbed	ended
puffed	bugged	disgusted
missed	saved	booted
wished	caused	.
.	budged	.
.	hummed	.
.	.	(etc.)
(etc.)	.	
	(etc.)	

3. The teacher may ask the class how they knew which endings go with which verbs. Some class members may begin to guess the right answer. Others may claim that they memorized the association for each individual verb. A further tactic will discredit the memorization theory: Providing a list of nonsense words, the teacher asks the class to imagine that these words are English verbs and to say them in the past tense. Again, the class unanimously chooses the appropriate form of the past tense. Obviously this choice cannot be attributed to memorization of individual associations since the students have never before heard the nonsense "verbs."

[-t]	[-d]	[-əd]
hoped	played	waited
dropped	died	confronted
.	.	.
.	.	.
.	.	.
(etc.)	(etc.)	(etc.)
slooped	loyed	olted
plassed	somed	grimpted
maffed	alved	gnaded
.	.	.
.	.	.
.	.	.
(etc.)	(etc.)	(etc.)

4. The teacher then reasks the question: What made you categorize these verbs as you did? What do the verbs in each category have in common? By this time hopefully some of the students will have noticed the recurrence of final letters or final sounds within groups. If necessary, the teacher can drop hints leading the students to a realization that the final sound of the verb determines the pronunciation of the past tense marker. Students can then construct a list of the final sounds preceding each of the three past tense markers.

[-t]	[-d]	[-əd]
[p], [k],	all vowel	[t], [d]
[f], [s],	sounds, [b],	
[š], [č]	[g], [v],	
	[z], [ð],	
	[j], [m],	
	[n], [ŋ],	
	[l], [r],	
	[y], [w]	

5. The teacher might at this point encourage the students to go further in their analysis by discovering that all of the sounds preceding the past tense pronunciation [-t] are voiceless (the vocal cords do not vibrate during their pronunciation) and all of the sounds preceding [-d] are voiced (the vocal cords do vibrate).

Finally, the students might consider the two exceptional sounds [t] and [d] which precede the third past tense marker [-əd]. Some students will realize that, without the vowel that comes between it and the preceding consonant, the past tense [-t] or [-d] could not be properly articulated in English.

Guided in this way students can derive the rules for the pronunciation of the regular past tense forms in English simply by considering their own speech; they can both supply and analyze the data themselves. As they do, they should come to recognize that, though they have just become able to state them formally, their speech has always followed rules of pronunciation. Seldom is the learner in a better position to provide himself with the information necessary to make inductive generalizations, and seldom are such generalizations as surprising and as pleasing.

▣ ▣ ▣

Good English—unless *good* is defined circularly as *that which the schools consider good*—is not necessarily taught in schools. Good English is English that communicates what the speaker intends to the audience he or she is trying to reach: the English labeled "good" by the schools is often not very useful in addressing the audiences the student is likely to encounter outside of school.

But imposing a system of artificial language norms within the classroom can have even more serious consequences: when their spoken or written language is constantly corrected, students may lose confidence in their ability to express themselves. As a parent-volunteer I once assisted a fourth-grade teacher who was taking her class on a tour of a tuna-processing plant. In the bus on the way home, following a morning of varied sights and pungent smells, each student was given a little notebook (with a picture of a tuna on the cover) and was asked to write a description of the trip. I shuddered inwardly in sympathy, but none of the children seemed to share my anxieties about writing. They simply sat in the bus and wrote until they had exhausted their interest in the subject or until the bus ride ended or until they fell asleep. Will those same students, by the time they finish high school, chew their pencils in terror at the sight of a blank sheet of paper? I fear that many will, and regret that part of the blame for this tragic loss of spontaneous verbalization will rest with their English teachers. I fear that teachers consciously teaching the joys of self-expression and the beauties of literature will unconsciously be teaching these other lessons:

LANGUAGE IS GOVERNED BY COMPLEX RULES WHICH YOU DO NOT KNOW AND WHICH YOU MUST LEARN BEFORE YOU CAN EXPRESS YOURSELF PROPERLY.

YOUR WRITING CONTAINS MANY MISTAKES WHICH YOU CANNOT RECOGNIZE.

THE MORE YOUR WRITING SOUNDS LIKE THE ADULT WHICH YOU ARE NOT, RATHER THAN THE CHILD OR ADOLESCENT WHICH YOU ARE, THE BETTER IT IS.

How widely such doctrines are accepted; yet how misguided they seem.

In a sense, the English teacher's job is ironic: he is teaching English to speakers of English—teaching a langauge to children or adults who already know that language and how to continue learning it. That is the most important message linguists have for English teachers. Taking this message to heart, the English teacher can design a curriculum that encourages and builds upon his students' natural language-learning abilities and upon the knowledge of language they already possess. He can help them expand their language capacities to include, in written as well as spoken expression, the words and verbal strategies demanded by ever-widening needs and audiences. He can, in addition, help his students become aware of and understand public opinion concerning language variation without at the same time becoming slaves to that opinion. And finally, the English teacher can, if he wishes, lead students to a conscious awareness of the language they already unconsciously command so that they may marvel at the complexity and beauty of its structure, its sounds, and its history.

DATE DUE

GAYLORD			PRINTED IN U.S.A.